A Sacred B

In the profound depths of a dimly lit room, I find myself encircled by seven companions, each on the threshold of a healing retreat. Our sanctuary is sealed with a protective prayer—a heartfelt plea to our healed ancestors for their wisdom and presence. We invite only love and positive intentions to envelop us throughout this sacred ceremony.

With a collective breath, we surrender ourselves to the mysteries of this journey. A peaceful aura fills the space, presided over by our gifted Shaman, whose melodies and instruments guide us through a delicate dance—between chaos and order, fear and courage, darkness and light, pain and pleasure. It is a journey of profound self-discovery.

This book is an invitation to embark on your own path of inner transformation, peeling back the layers to reveal the truth of your worthiness and untapped potential. The world—abundant, alive, and waiting—is yours to embrace.

In humble dedication, I offer this work to the countless souls trapped in the web of human trafficking. May the words within serve as a beacon of peace, love, and cooperation for all of humanity.

"This memory from a sacred healing retreat remains etched in my soul. It helped me to give greater depth to the chapters that you're about to read."

The Path Ahead

Discover Who You Are
and What You Want in Life

PUBLISHED BY; DEVLIN TIKITIKI

The Path Ahead

First Edition, May 2025
Publisher: Tūwhitia Press

ISBN: 9798283293158

TABLE OF CONTENTS

Introduction

Welcome, my friend—and congratulations on choosing to elevate your life. Whether your goals involve wealth, health, love, relationships, or happiness, this book will remind you of the power already within you and how to use it to create the life you dream of.

In today's fast-paced world, it's easy to excel in one area while struggling in others. This imbalance often stems from a lack of personal growth and mindfulness—two essential elements for harmony across all areas of life. When embraced, they lead to stronger relationships, better mental health, and a more fulfilling, balanced existence.

As Lewis Howes, host of *The School of Greatness* and a leading voice in men's personal development, says: **"When we ignore emotional growth, it doesn't matter how much success we have—our relationships and inner peace suffer."**

Introduction

Whether you're a high-powered executive, a dedicated professional, or someone committed to living a better life, the principles in this book are designed to help you navigate and improve both your personal and professional relationships.

The Path Ahead: *Discover Who You Are and What You Want in Life* delves into the essential elements of personal growth and self-discovery, guiding you through understanding your purpose, identity, and the world around you. It addresses the impact of fears, trauma, and relationships on our lives, offering insights into healing and building character. Additionally, this book explores the power of language, goal-setting, and visualization techniques to help you shape a fulfilling future.

Discovering the real, authentic you can lead to becoming a different version of yourself—one who is open, resilient, and ready to embrace all that life has to offer. I am thrilled you picked up this book because it tells me you are curious about what else life has to offer. Whatever your reason for starting this journey, I trust this book will serve you well.

Reflect on these questions as you begin:

- What matters most to you?
- What do you desire?
- What do you want to change in your life?

The Path Ahead

A lot of people today are investing in their health and well-being, seeking mindful practices, and looking for ways to connect meaningfully with themselves, the environment, and others. As a society, we are increasingly stressed, disconnected, and anxious, leading to a rise in mental health issues, eating disorders, and a troubling increase in youth suicide. We all yearn for happiness. It's time to stop suffering.

The Path Ahead: *Discover Who You Are and What You Want in Life* is about aligning with your core values and beliefs, exploring your purpose, identifying and utilizing your strengths, and falling in love with yourself again. It's about understanding what truly matters to you and envisioning your ideal future and self.

Take a moment to consider what is your ideal lifestyle and future.

- What type of person do you want to be?

- Where do you live, and what are you doing?

- Who do you spend your time with?

Perhaps you want to have more fun, work less, and fully enjoy quality time with your partner and children. Maybe you want to express more love to and be open to receiving love in return. Or perhaps you feel disconnected from yourself and are seeking to fall back in love with who you are.

Introduction

The Path Ahead: *Discover Who You Are and What You Want in Life* is here to remind you of your worth, that you matter, that you can be happier, and that you are enough. This way of living, which I call being the 'Ultimate You,' is about becoming your ideal self on your terms. if you feel something needs to change in your life, reading this book is a great start.

This book is the culmination of my journey and what I've learned about tapping into the resources we all possess. It is designed to help you transform your life by exploring methods, tools, and resources from experts in personal development, spirituality, mindset growth, and neurolinguistics. I also share insights from experiences with ancient medicines and healing retreats.

Writing this book has been a joyous process, despite the challenges of life, COVID, lifestyle changes, and procrastination getting in the way. I share some of my personal stories and experiences throughout the chapters to take you on my journey—from overcoming the odds of growing up in poverty, surviving child abuse, and dropping out of school, to conquering toxic habits, living a life of abundance, being an educator, and finding fulfillment.

I am clear on what I want and live with purpose, experiencing each day with love, compassion, and fulfillment at one of the most beautiful cities in the world—Sydney, Australia.

The Path Ahead

This book includes questions, reflections, activities, and online links to further your education alongside the content. It will help you start mapping out your aspirations and dreams. While it may not provide all the answers, it is a great start for your journey of growth or, at the very least, an incredible read. Is now the time to open your mind and live a life of abundance and peace?

How It All Started for Me: My Own Transformation

In 2009, at the age of 30, I was disconnected from who I was. I had no clear vision for my future and was on a path of perpetual self-destruction. I was a binge drinker, filled with anger and resentment, allowing marijuana to rule my life and suppress my shame.

I had lived my whole adult life up to this point pretending everything was okay, when in reality, my life was going nowhere. I was unhappy, often depressed, and silently miserable. I was overweight and disliked who I saw in the mirror. My self-esteem was low, and I masked this by being a people-pleaser, putting others' needs before my own. I was clueless about the unlimited potential sitting dormant inside me. Deep down, like many others, I knew there had to be more to life than this. The story I kept telling myself was that I wasn't good enough or worthy of anything better.

Introduction

In September of 2009, I attended a three-day Breakthrough To Success seminar with Christopher Howard, an NLP and transformational life coach. At this seminar, I realized I was holding myself back from abundant opportunities and increased growth. I saw that I was living as an imposter, being someone I was not. I was introduced to tools and resources that changed my thinking. I wanted a life of happiness and fulfillment instead of being unhappy and fake. I started to see my unlimited potential and felt a 10-tonne load lifted off my shoulders. I had a paradigm shift and I was transformed.

From this moment, I developed a profound interest in mindset growth, human behavior, and personal development. For the next fourteen years, I immersed myself in personal growth seminars, NLP courses, sales and marketing training, networking events, and a wealth of books and videos on self-help and mindset. I listened to countless hours of podcasts and studied the principles of personal development.

This journey led me to resign from my secure corporate job in finance to become a mindset mastery life coach, establish my own businesses, and publish this book.

"If you change the way you look at things, the things you look at change."
—Dr. Wayne Dyer

When You Change How You See Yourself, The World Around You Changes:

One of my favourite stories, because of its incredibility, is about the transformation I experienced just months after attending that life-changing seminar. I went from living in a run-down hostel with rats running through it to living on a Princess Cruise Ship as an officer, traveling the world. With less than $50 in my pocket, I embarked on the Sun Princess, traveling the seas in luxury, dining in fine settings every evening, and being spoiled with majestic views all around the world. I had shifted from a mindset of scarcity to one of abundance, and everything changed.

Weeks after my transformation, I was unfairly fired from my hostel reception job. While searching for a new opportunity, I came across an opening for a Junior Assistant Cruise Director position with Princess Cruises. Despite having no experience or qualifications in Tourism and Hospitality, I believed I was worthy and capable of this position. The previous version of me would have made every excuse, but the transformed me saw this as the perfect opportunity.

When I saw the job vacancy, I felt as if I had already been offered the position. I believed with every fibre of my being that this was meant for me. I visualized myself in this new role, felt the excitement, and knew deep down that I was about to embark on something extraordinary.

Introduction

I researched the role of a Junior Assistant Cruise Director, learning about the destinations I would visit on my first six-month contract, including countries like Rabaul, Maldives, Seychelles, China, India, Thailand, Mauritius, and South Africa. I was open and accepting of this incredible opportunity. To add to this remarkable event, I was promoted to Assistant Cruise Director during my job interview—a promotion that included a higher officer ranking, my own suite, and an increased salary.

This was just the beginning of numerous opportunities and magnificent experiences that continue to come my way. Because I changed how I saw myself, the way I saw the world changed instantly. I no longer feared what people thought of me. I replaced a limiting belief that had me fearing judgment with a resourceful belief that no one cares about what I do, so I should go for it. I developed an insatiable curiosity about quantum physics, the power of the mind, and the law of attraction. More importantly, I believed in my own unlimited potential. As Henry Ford said, *"Whether you think you can, or whether you think you can't, either way, you are right."* I now believed that "I CAN" do whatever I set my mind to (and so can you)!

Let this be a courageous stepping stone for you to create the change that you know is possible.

The Path Ahead

Questions for you to answer.

What change deep down inside of <u>you</u> do you know needs to be made and what would that be?

1. Now imagine for a moment that if you were to make that change how much better would your life be?

2. What are the feelings associated to that moment and what would you say to yourself once you achieve that change?

3. And, then think, if you were to stay the same way without the change, what will it cost you and the other people in your life?

Take a moment to answer the questions above before moving forward. This journey isn't one to rush. I encourage you to pause and reflect on each question, allowing yourself the time to truly think and absorb. Rather than speeding through the content, savour the moments of self-discovery and insight.

As you continue reading, remember to do the same whenever a question is posed. Let each question be an opportunity for reflection, growth, and deeper understanding. The more you engage with these moments, the more meaningful this journey will be.

Once again my friend, welcome and congratulations on making the decision to explore how you can elevate your life… See you on the other side.

CHAPTER ONE

Purpose

Navigating Your Path

"The fact is, you are here to meet a need of someone or something."
- Jim Rohn

Knowing Your Purpose

Purpose drives, anchors, and motivates us, infusing our lives with meaning. It is the lens through which we understand our place in the world and how we contribute to it. Purpose encourages us to rediscover parts of ourselves that may have been forgotten and guides us to become the person we are meant to be. Finding meaning in your life starts with recognizing that you matter and belong in this world.

As we explore throughout this chapter, identifying and pursuing your purpose is the foundation of a fulfilling life. However, understanding your true purpose requires commitment and introspection, as it involves making sense of how you fit into the broader world around you

The Path Ahead

You must devote time to yourself, just as you do for others. While this process can be confronting, it is essential for personal growth.

Our true purpose begins with knowing ourselves deeply, which means understanding our thoughts, emotions, and past experiences. You can't truly know who you are without acknowledging what has shaped you—including the unpleasant experiences. The first step is self-awareness because you can only love others to the extent that you love yourself. This self-awareness also extends to understanding your place in the world and how your actions impact those around you.

Living in alignment with your purpose brings richness, depth, and happiness to life. You'll feel "in flow," where opportunities, people, and events seem to fall into place, as if you attracted them. Even in tough times, fortunate outcomes will remind you of the importance of faith, hope, and optimism—attributes essential for navigating life.

For some, purpose is equated with success, but what does success truly mean? Many believe it involves wealth and a carefree life, but endless vacationing would soon grow tedious. This is because, at our core, we seek significance—a need that goes unmet in superficial pursuits. True purpose remains constant, even when external circumstances change.

Purpose

Real success is an inner feeling. It's about who you are, not what you possess. The wealthiest people often grapple with unhappiness, depression, and failed relationships. Money doesn't buy happiness.

Reinventing Myself: From Adversity to Empowerment

In 2019, after years of personal growth and education, I decided to become a certified NLP practitioner and to study and become a Mindset Mastery Life Coach. This led to a deeper understanding of my purpose. Living with purpose allows me to face challenges with grace and resilience, knowing I'm working toward something bigger than myself.

During the pandemic in 2020, when many people struggled with anxiety and fear, I chose self-reinvention. I prioritized my health, gave up harmful habits, and established new routines that enhanced my well-being by using tools that I had studied through the life coaching training. These changes helped me cope with adversity, and I became stronger and more resilient. I embraced spiritual growth, deepening my understanding of myself and the world.

Using these experiences, I began coaching others, aligning with the vision I had for myself years earlier. The journey wasn't easy, but purpose made it more fulfilling.

Understanding Your Values

Understanding your values is crucial to aligning with your purpose. Values serve as your personal compass, guiding you through difficult decisions and keeping you grounded in what truly matters. When your actions are in harmony with your values, you experience greater fulfillment, clarity, and a stronger sense of integrity. This alignment empowers you to live more authentically and confidently navigate life's challenges.

Without a clear understanding of your values, it's easy to feel lost or pulled in different directions. In Chapter Three: *Identity*, we will explore beliefs and values in greater depth, helping you further solidify your connection to your purpose.

The Evolving Nature of Purpose

Your purpose may evolve as you grow and experience new things. What drives you today may change as you learn more about yourself and the world. It's important to stay open and flexible, allowing your purpose to develop naturally over time. Trust that each stage of your journey brings you closer to the person you're meant to become. As you encounter new experiences, relationships, and insights, your understanding of your purpose may deepen or shift. This evolution is not a sign of instability but of growth and self-awareness. Embrace the changes as part of your transformation into a fuller, more authentic version of yourself.

Purpose

Uncover Your Why

Positive psychology suggests that understanding your purpose is key to mental wellness. It gives you a sense of how you fit into the world. Ignoring your purpose can lead to depression, addiction, and dissatisfaction. A lack of purpose can also impact your health and relationships, pulling you away from the person you're meant to be.

Many people go through life unaware disconnected from their full potential and deeper truths. Being unaware often manifests in limiting beliefs and self-destructive behaviors. As Indian spiritual teacher Sadhguru says, *"People are slowly dying rather than living the rest of their life."*

Unawareness traps people in cycles of fear, dissatisfaction, and unhealthy habits. I know this because I've been there before living without purpose. Not everyone needs a defined purpose to be content, but if you feel that something is missing, you're in the right place to explore that.

One common self-sabotaging behavior is repeating the same actions while expecting different results. As Einstein said, this is the definition of insanity. Often, this cycle is driven by boredom—an indication that life lacks meaning or purpose. We've grown impatient in our fast-paced world, seeking instant gratification. When inconveniences arise, it frustrates us. Yet, this impatience disconnects us from the present moment and deepens our discomfort with silence, waiting, and boredom.

To move beyond boredom and uncover a deeper sense of purpose, consider the following:

1. **Dare to be your authentic self.**

2. **Discover yourself by helping others.**

3. **Turn obstacles into opportunities.**

1. Dare to Be the Authentic You

Authenticity requires honesty with yourself. Are you longing for change but stuck in old habits? Being authentic means embracing who you are and letting go of the need for external approval. It demands courage to stand by your values and beliefs without worrying about what others think.

"True belonging only happens when we present our authentic, imperfect selves to the world. Our sense of belonging can never be greater than our level of self-acceptance." - Brené Brown

Embracing authenticity means confronting the parts of yourself you've been ashamed of and releasing outdated habits. You need a clear vision of who you want to become, an understanding of your strengths, and mindfulness of your thoughts. This awareness empowers you to make intentional, goal-oriented decisions, even when faced with challenges. It's not easy to let go of the parts of yourself that no longer serve you, but this is essential for growth.

Secondary gain—when a negative habit offers comfort despite holding you back—can be particularly challenging to overcome.

These comforts, like addiction or self-sabotage, may feel good in the moment but ultimately stunt your growth. As we shed these old habits, we might reflect on Pinocchio's realization: "How foolish I was when I was a puppet." Similarly, we often allow others or societal expectations to control us. Authentic living means taking control and aligning your actions with your true values and desires.

2. Discovering Yourself by Helping Others

"When we learn to care about others, we worry less about ourselves."

Serving others is one of the most profound ways to discover yourself. It gives you a sense of significance—one of the six core human needs identified by life coach Tony Robbins. Significance stems from contributing to the world, which enriches your spirit and helps you realize your value. Focusing on others instead of yourself creates deeper meaning and purpose. For instance, setting a goal to improve your health not only benefits you but also benefits your family.

Your actions can have a ripple effect, inspiring and uplifting others. Similarly, mentoring a colleague at work not only helps them grow professionally but also enhances the overall team's performance and morale, creating a more positive and productive work environment. In a world filled with division, we need more love, cooperation, and respect. As Robert Ingersoll said, *"We rise by lifting others."* When you shift your focus toward helping others, you'll find greater fulfillment in your actions.

Practical Tool:

Consider keeping a journal where you reflect on how your actions contribute to the well-being of others. Ask yourself, "What can I do today to align more closely with my purpose and help someone else?" This daily reflection reinforces your commitment to living purposefully.

3. Turning Obstacles into Opportunities

Obstacles often feel uncomfortable because they expose our vulnerabilities. Yet, they teach us valuable lessons and prepare us for future challenges. Overcoming adversity builds resilience, strength, and skills, which are critical to personal growth.

Embracing challenges helps you appreciate the journey and recognize that obstacles are a necessary part of progress. Life's greatest lessons often come from moments of pain, regret, or disappointment. Successful people see obstacles as opportunities to learn and grow.

"Obstacles are a sign you're doing something you care about and that matters to you." - - Sharon Pearson

Practical Tool:

Next time you face a challenge, ask yourself, "What is this teaching me?" Reflect on your answer and consider how overcoming this obstacle brings you closer to your goals.

The Power of Gratitude

Gratitude plays an important role in living with purpose. When we take time to appreciate the good things in our lives, we foster a sense of abundance and positivity.

Purpose

Cultivating gratitude helps us stay focused on what truly matters, grounding us in the present and making our pursuit of purpose more fulfilling.

Taking regular moments to express gratitude—whether through journaling, meditation, or simply reflecting on the people and experiences that have enriched your life—can reinforce your sense of purpose. When you live with gratitude, you open your heart to greater joy, contentment, and alignment with your purpose.

Practical Tool:

At the end of each day, write down three things you are grateful for. Consider how each of these contributes to your personal growth or connects with your purpose. This simple practice helps shift your mindset toward abundance, allowing you to approach life with a more positive and purposeful outlook.

When You Operate from Strengths vs. Weaknesses

When you're using your strengths, you feel energized, engaged, and confident. Tasks that align with your strengths often feel more effortless and enjoyable. For example, if one of your strengths is **creativity**, you might find yourself thriving in environments where problem-solving, brainstorming, or innovation is needed. You'll notice a natural flow when creating new ideas or solutions, and you'll feel fulfilled by the process.

On the other hand, if you're primarily focused on areas of weakness, you may feel drained or frustrated. Let's say one of your weaknesses is attention to detail. If your daily tasks require you to scrutinize minutiae for hours, you might feel exhausted, and the quality of your work may suffer.

You might even start doubting yourself or feeling inadequate, which can hinder your motivation and productivity. For instance, consider a person whose strength is **empathy** but is constantly placed in situations that demand intense logical analysis without much human interaction. Over time, they may feel disconnected or even question their capabilities, despite being naturally gifted in understanding and relating to people. On the flip side, if they work in a role that allows them to help others or connect on a deeper emotional level, such as counselling or team-building, they will likely thrive and feel deeply fulfilled.

Leveraging Your Strengths for Success

By understanding your strengths, you can intentionally seek out opportunities that play to those abilities. Knowing your strengths allows you to align with opportunities where you naturally excel. Too often, we focus on weaknesses instead of leveraging our unique talents.

For example, if your strength is **leadership**, you might excel in roles that require guiding teams, making decisions, or inspiring others. In contrast, focusing on areas of weakness, like introversion in a high-pressure public-speaking role, might result in stress and dissatisfaction, despite all efforts to improve.

Knowing your strengths is not about avoiding weaknesses but about emphasizing what makes you naturally strong. By aligning your daily actions and decisions with your strengths, you set yourself up for success, personal satisfaction, and long-term growth. Embracing your unique strengths allows you to contribute to the world in the most authentic and effective way.

Purpose

Research shows that using your strengths makes you 18 times more likely to flourish. Everyone has a unique blend of strengths. Embracing your individuality and celebrating your diversity leads to personal growth and fulfillment. Psychologist Martin Seligman identified six core virtues common across many traditions: You can discover more of his work in the link provided below. To discover your strengths, take the **free** VIA Character Survey at viacharacter.org. This scientifically backed assessment helps you identify your unique character strengths, which are essential for aligning with your purpose and flourishing in life.

The results will be sent directly to your email, providing you with valuable insights that you can use to maximize your potential and create a more meaningful, purpose-driven life.

Conclusion Understanding your purpose is just the first step on the journey to a fulfilling life. The next challenge is aligning your daily actions with that purpose and to live the life you really want. In later chapters, we'll explore essential tools like goal-setting and visualization to help you bring your vision to life. But before diving into those techniques, it's important to focus on a key element that influences everything: your perspective. In Chapter Two, we will explore how your perception shapes your reality and how it can either support or undermine your purpose.

By mastering the art of perspective, you will gain the clarity and focus needed to stay aligned with your purpose, regardless of the obstacles that arise.

CHAPTER TWO

Perspective

Embracing New Views of the World

"It isn't the event that stresses you out but the meaning you put to it".

— Tony Robbins

You Create Your Own Reality

In this chapter, you'll uncover how your perception shapes your reality and learn how to harness this power to transform your life. We'll dive into the science behind your brain's filtering system, explore how to shift your responses to serve you better, and reveal why your focus directs your energy. This knowledge is the key to creating your own reality. Steven Covey, the influential author of *"The 7 Habits of Highly Effective People,"* once said, "We don't see the world as it is, we see the world as we are." Covey's statement highlights a powerful truth: our self-perception shapes our view of the world. When you see yourself as full of potential and opportunity, the world reflects that back to you. But this isn't just a matter of mood; it's about consciously choosing a response that puts you in a favorable state of being.

Perspective

Neuroscience and personal development both affirm that while we can't change external factors like the weather, politics, pandemics, death, or other people's reactions, we can control how we respond to these situations. Even in circumstances beyond our control, like a natural disaster, we retain the power to choose our reaction.

Will you rise and find solutions, or will you succumb to the role of the victim?

Indeed, Allah will not change the condition of a people until they change what is in themselves. - (Surah Ar-Ra'd, 13:11)

Often, the results we experience in life are directly linked to our own actions and reactions, a truth that can be challenging to accept. Maya Angelou, the revered American memoirist and civil rights activist, wisely said, *"If you are unhappy with the results, then change them, and if you can't change them, change your attitude."*

To bring about change in your life, you must first understand the interconnectedness of your thoughts, emotions, and behaviors.

These elements follow a specific pattern, leading to outcomes that shape your experience of the world. If you're not satisfied with a result, shift your perception. The way you view things can change in an instant, depending on how you choose to react.

Ask yourself: could I have done something differently to achieve a better outcome? Sometimes, the result we get is exactly what we expected not necessarily what we needed. As Tony Robbins famously said, *"If you do not like the result, then change the process."*

Your Perception

You have the power to change an outcome by examining and altering the process, and it all starts with your perception. Perception is the ability to see, hear, or become aware of something through your senses. It differs from perspective, which is your attitude or way of regarding something—in other words, your point of view. It's essential to maintain a healthy perception because it filters your experience of the world.

Your perception plays a crucial role in determining the meaning of events and how you feel about them, which in turn shapes the quality of your experiences. If your perception is undesirable, your experience of the world will be undesirable.

Every result in your life begins with how you perceive external events, whether it's attending a friend's wedding, enjoying a meal at a restaurant, witnessing the birth of your first child, receiving upsetting news, or even facing a significant loss like a job or a loved one. Each event serves as a stimulus, and you assign it meaning through your internal dialogue—your thoughts.

Perspective

These thoughts are based on your perception of yourself and the world around you. For example, the birth of a child might bring immense joy to someone who has eagerly anticipated starting a family, while it could evoke anxiety in another person concerned about the responsibilities of parenthood in an uncertain world. These contrasting feelings can even coexist within the same set of parents. If you placed ten people in a room, each would have a unique perspective on childbirth and parenting.

Your Experience of the Past

The meaning you assign to your thoughts generates corresponding emotions—whether anger, rejection, happiness, ecstasy, or fear. These emotions, in turn, influence your actions and behaviors, setting your energy and frequency, and ultimately attracting more of the same into your life. Consider the two parents mentioned earlier: one feels joy and acts positively, while the other feels stressed and acts cautiously.

Their differing emotions and actions create distinct physical sensations in their bodies, leading to vastly different experiences. You choose your experience by the meaning you assign to an event and how you respond. The feelings that arise from this meaning dictate how you experience the world. If your experience is poor, it's often because your perception is poor. Conversely, if your perception is empowering, your experience will be as well.

The Path Ahead

Imagine someone wrongs you. If you choose to forgive, you'll experience feelings of peace, calm, and love. But if you hold a grudge, you'll harbor anger, tension, and stress. Let me share a personal example of how changing my perspective instantly transformed my feelings about a situation.

Once, while waiting to board a bus, I grew impatient with a passenger who was taking longer than usual to get off. I was bothered with the thought why he hadn't prepared his transport card in advance to avoid delaying us. But then I noticed he was struggling with a large bag in his left hand and crutches under his right arm due to an leg injury. My impatience and annoyance quickly turned into patience and empathy. By shifting my perspective, I changed my feelings from tension to relax. This experience illustrates the power of mastering your mind by choosing a perspective that fosters uplifting emotions.

It's about consciously selecting the feelings you prefer to have and recognizing that it all starts with your thoughts—something only you can control.

We cannot change anything outside of ourselves except for the way we perceive it. Picture yourself in my situation. Would you feel annoyed and frustrated with the person taking a long time to get off the bus, or would you choose to be understanding and patient? What can you learn from this example?

The Power of Perception and Focus

Our brains constantly process an overwhelming amount of information from the world around us, but we only pay attention to a small fraction of it. This is where the Reticular Activating System (RAS) comes in. Think of it as your brain's filter, deciding what's important based on your beliefs, values, and current focus.

What you focus on most becomes your reality. If you constantly think about problems, your RAS will highlight more evidence of the problem(s). But if you focus on solutions, you'll start seeing opportunities everywhere. This selective attention is what drives the law of attraction, where your energy flows towards what you concentrate on. Vision boards, for instance, are a practical tool that taps into this mechanism. By visualizing your goals, you program your RAS to notice opportunities that align with what you want. It's like tuning your mental radio to the right station—suddenly, you hear the music that's been playing all along.

Imagine being at a party with several conversations happening simultaneously. Suddenly, you hear your name from across the room. Your focus shifts immediately because the RAS has flagged that information as important. The RAS is also responsible for someone's ability to sleep through traffic noise but wake up at the smallest cry from their infant child.

Another example is when you buy a new bag or piece of clothing and then suddenly notice many others with the same item, even though you hadn't seen it before.

The RAS Effect: Shaping Your Reality Through Focus

The RAS can't distinguish between a real event and a contrived reality, so we can program it to seek out stimuli that resonate with our goals. Getting a clear picture in your mind of what you want is one way to program the RAS, but creating a vision board is even more effective. A vision board programs the RAS to pay attention to things in your environment that align with your goals, much like how you can pick up your name in a conversation across the room. This selective attention filter makes you aware of daily opportunities that can help you achieve your goals, and it's your job to act on those opportunities when they present themselves.

Tony Robbins aptly summarizes this concept with the phrase, *"Your energy flows where your focus goes."* This means that if you focus on problems, you will see more problems, but if you focus on solutions, you will find more solutions.

Mastering your mind involves choosing a perspective that fosters positive physiological feelings. By consciously selecting your thoughts and focusing on what you want, you can create a reality that aligns with your aspirations and desires.

Perspective

Perception is the ability to see, hear, or become aware of something through our senses. This differs from perspective, which is a particular attitude or way of regarding something—in other words, a point of view. It's crucial to maintain a healthy perception because our experience of the world is filtered through it.

1. An event takes place - the situation / stimulus
2. Your self-talk - (thoughts) = *meaning that you put to the event*
3. Your feelings – (emotions) = *comes from your perception of the event*
4. Your behaviours – (actions) = *you either respond or you react*
5. The experience – (outcome) = *favourable or unfavourable*

Perception is Reality: Shifting Focus to Break Limitations

Your focus is crucial because it directly influences the results you experience in life. To change focus is to break the barriers of conditional thinking and limited beliefs that distort our view of the world. Do you choose to see opportunities and solutions, or do you choose to see obstacles and problems. If you focus on the solution, you will start to attract everything related to that solution. Conversely, if you focus on the problem, you will attract more of the problem. People who focus on problems limit their opportunities. The universe interprets their focus as a desire for more problems and thus provides them.

They accumulate evidence to believe there's no way out, convincing themselves they've tried everything or that the problem is unsolvable.

Carl Jung a Swiss psychiatrist and psychoanalyst who founded analytical psychology believed that we can't see anything outside of us that isn't within us, aligning with the idea that we don't see things as they are, but as we are.

We only know what we know and experience what we search for; everything else is outside our experience. However, if our imaginative minds can create such outcomes by focusing on problems, is it possible that focusing on solutions could yield the opposite result? Of course it would, right?

Your Mind's Power: Align with What You Truly Want

Research shows that we are masses of energy emitting transmissions into the world, and our thoughts play a critical role in shaping our experiences. In the same way, spiritual teachings remind us that our thoughts and intentions align with divine will, influencing the outcomes in our lives.

Bob Proctor, a renowned motivational speaker, author, and success coach, emphasized the idea that "like attracts like"—that our thoughts become things. This resonates with the concept that our intentions, when aligned with faith and the divine, set the course for our life's journey. Many people are more adept at identifying what they don't want rather than focusing on what they do.

However, in both spiritual practice and psychology, we learn that the mind doesn't recognize negations like "no" or "don't.".

For instance, if you say, "I don't want to be anxious," your mind registers, "I want to be anxious.". In Islam, it is taught to focus on positive intentions and trust in Allah's plan, believing that what we seek will be granted if it is good for us. It is important to reframe your thoughts to affirm what you desire. Instead of saying, "I don't want this addiction," say, "I seek to live a healthy, sober life." This way, your focus shifts toward what is in alignment with divine will and positive transformation. As the Qur'an teaches, *"Verily, Allah does not change the condition of a people until they change what is in themselves"* (Qur'an, 13:11).

Through faith, positive thought, and aligning our desires with what is best for us, we can bring about lasting change. The good news is that it's never too late to shift your mindset, align with your purpose, and start over. Trust in God's wisdom, believe in the power of your thoughts, and act in harmony with both to create the reality you truly seek.

Feelings of appreciation

You will notice this topic will appear several times throughout this book. The solution is to focus on feelings of gratitude or appreciation. When we appreciate something about a situation, the fear related to it starts to disappear.

Fear and appreciation are accessed in different parts of the brain, so you can't feel both emotions simultaneously. Focusing on gratitude shifts your perspective and attracts positive experiences.

To focus on appreciation is to exclude what you fear, then fear decreases.

To focus on fear is to exclude what you're able, and capable of.

Where are you choosing to focus on, and is that focus working for you?

Is your focus getting you the results you are seeking?

What Your Focus on Is What You Get

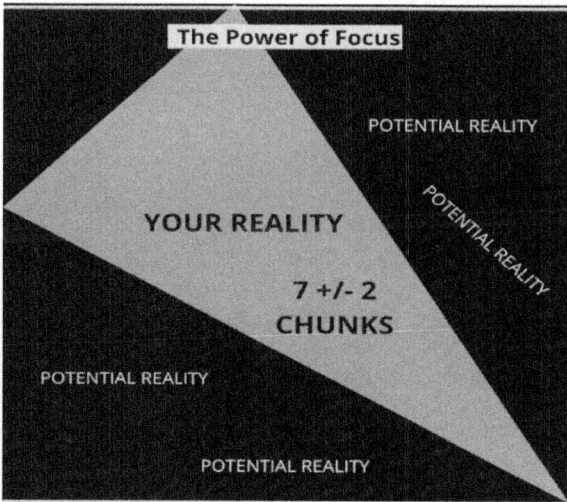

Perspective

Using the 'Power of Focus' diagram, the triangle represents our focus, defining our reality. Everything within this region is captured, while everything outside of it is excluded. We can't perceive what we don't focus on, and similarly, we remain unaware of what we don't know until we expand our awareness. So the principle is 'what you focus on is what you get at the exemption of everything else. Research into the power of focus highlights its significant impact on our experiences and outcomes. The principle that "where attention goes, energy flows" suggests that by purposefully directing our focus, we can lead more fulfilling and successful lives.

By concentrating on what truly matters—be it personal goals, professional endeavors, or nurturing relationships—we can channel our energy more effectively and enhance our efforts. Mindfulness practices, such as meditation, support this by training us to stay present and direct our attention intentionally. This helps create a positive ripple effect in our lives, as our focused attention amplifies our actions and propels us forward. Additionally, focusing our attention intentionally is crucial for living a purposeful life. When we concentrate on positive thoughts, actions, and goals, we foster an environment conducive to growth and resilience. This approach can be transformative, especially during challenging times, as it encourages us to maintain a focus on gratitude and positive outcomes.

By directing our energy towards our intentions rather than distractions, we can cultivate a more rewarding existence, ultimately shaping a reality that aligns with our aspirations and desires. This conscious management of our attention not only improves our mental and emotional well-being but also enhances our ability to achieve our goals and create a meaningful life.

Your Awareness to Discover the unknown

The following steps and questions can help you shift your perspective and expand your awareness to find the answers you need:

Tip: When you have hit a boundary in your focus or thinking. Ask yourself questions that will stretch your thinking because it is only in the realm of what you don't know that the magic will happen, and you start to experience different results.

- If someone who you care for and love a lot had the same problem as you, what advice would you give them?

- In what ways can you follow your own advice in this example?

- If it was possible to look at the situation in a positive way, what would that be?

- What are the possibilities here? What else is there?

- How can you turn things around and what would be the first step?

Conclusion:

As we conclude this chapter on perspective, it's important to remember that the way you perceive the world fundamentally shapes your reality.Your perspective not only influences your emotions but also determines the outcomes you attract into your life. By consciously focusing on solutions, opportunities, and positive outcomes, you gain the power to transform your experiences and, ultimately, your reality.

The insights you've gained—understanding your brain's filtering system and the profound impact of your focus—are invaluable tools for navigating life with clarity and purpose.

The energy you project into the world shapes the life you live, and by honing your focus on what truly matters, you can align your life with your deepest aspirations. As you move forward, continue to ask yourself: *Where am I placing my focus, and how is it shaping my experience?* These reflections will guide you toward a more intentional and fulfilling life.

However, perspective is only part of the equation. As we transition into **Chapter Three**, we'll delve into the depths of your *identity—examining your self-perception,* beliefs, and values form the foundation of who you are. Understanding your identity is crucial for living authentically and aligning your actions with your true self.

The Path Ahead

In this next chapter, we will explore how to ground your self-view in positivity, confront limiting beliefs, and connect with your true nature, so you can live a life that reflects your most genuine aspirations.

To help you continue this journey of self-discovery, we're offering a free activity booklet on creating a vision board. Email us at info@thepathahead.com.au to receive your copy and start shaping your vision for the future.

CHAPTER THREE

Identity

A Journey Within

"To be yourself in a world that is constantly trying to make you something else is the greatest accomplishment" - Ralph Waldo Emerson

Exploring The Depths of Your Identity

In this chapter, we'll explore the layers of your identity and how your self-perception, beliefs, and values influence the decisions you make. These elements are essential for constructing the ideal lifestyle and future you aspire to, particularly in today's world, where distractions and noise are pervasive.

By focusing on a positive self-view, you can recognize how key moments in your life have shaped limiting beliefs that may either hold you back or drive you toward the changes you desire. I have also included something very special for you in this chapter—a glimpse into Māori philosophy regarding identity.

They descended from the Polynesian people who arrived in Aotearoa New Zealand around the 13th century, navigating vast oceans using sophisticated canoes and stellar navigation. Māori society is organized into iwi (tribes) and hapū (sub-tribes), each with its own distinct history and customs. As a Māori descendant of Ngati Porou and Rongowhakaata, my heritage is deeply rooted in the East Coast of New Zealand's North Island. This ancestry connects me to a lineage of warriors, navigators, and storytellers, and informs my sense of identity and purpose. Māori philosophy helps us appreciate the importance of understanding our identity, connecting us to our roots, values, and the stories of our ancestors. Embrace your authentic self, and let your true nature guide you toward the fulfilling life you deserve. Your journey is unique, and with the right mindset, you can achieve remarkable things.

Discovering Your True Identity

Have you ever felt like you're pretending to be someone you're not or that a vital part of you is missing? When you live authentically, you'll find that everything around you flows more smoothly.

True success stems from being your authentic self. If you're constantly concealing your true nature, you'll never realize your full potential. Understanding who you are involves connecting with your true self and cultivating a healthy, positive belief in your identity, self-perception, and self-image. You must shine in the areas where you excel, rather than exhausting yourself by trying to meet the expectations and standards set by others.

Identity

Self-Reflection Questions:

- When do you feel most like yourself? What activities, environments, or people allow you to express your true identity?

- In what ways have you been compromising your authenticity to meet the expectations of others?

Charles Cooley, a sociologist, once wrote, *"I am not what I think I am, and I am not what you think I am. I am what I think you think I am."* Many people spend their entire lives striving to become the person they believe others want them to be, rather than who they genuinely wish to be. This often leads to feelings of inadequacy and impostor syndrome.

The fear of judgment or criticism prevents them from achieving their goals, causing them to take their dreams to the grave. There is a saying that the graveyard is the wealthiest place on the planet because so many people die with unfulfilled dreams and aspirations.................. Don't let that be your fate!

Brian Tracy, a renowned motivational speaker and self-development author, points out that negative emotions stem from the fear of loss, rejection, or criticism. By improving your self-image, self-perception, and self-esteem in ways that benefit you, you can overcome these negative emotions and live a more fulfilling life. Often, the perception you have of yourself does not align with your true identity.

This self-perception is typically shaped by past hurts and shame, creating an image that is not the real you but rather an imagined version. Your self-concept—who you think you should be—is frequently moulded by how you believe others perceive you. As a result, you may spend much of your life trying to meet the standards of others instead of your own.

Over time, your external reality mirrors your internal thoughts. This is why building self-esteem, and a positive self-image is crucial for personal growth. Self-esteem reflects how much you like yourself, which in turn shapes your self-image.

Self-Reflection Questions:

- How do you perceive yourself, and how does this perception align with who you truly are?
- What steps can you take to build a more positive and authentic self-image?

Māori Philosophy on Identity

Māori philosophy offers profound insights into understanding one's identity, deeply rooted in the concept of whakapapa a web of connections that links individuals to their ancestors, the land, and the wider community. In Māori culture, understanding one's identity starts with knowing where you come from. This connection to ancestry provides a sense of belonging and purpose. The land (whenua) is not just a place but a living entity that holds the history and stories of one's people.

Identity

Through whakapapa, individuals learn about their strengths, values, and the roles their ancestors played, which in turn shapes their own identity and sense of self. For example, Māori might trace their lineage back to a renowned navigator who guided their people across vast oceans. This ancestral story can instil a sense of resilience, courage, and leadership in the individual, qualities that become integral to their identity. By embracing the Māori concept of whakapapa, we can all deepen our understanding of who we are. It teaches us that our identity is multifaceted, influenced by our heritage, our connection to the land, and the communities we are part of. Recognizing and honoring these connections can help us understand our strengths and values, providing a clearer sense of who we are and our place in the world. By understanding these elements, we can cultivate a strong sense of identity that guides us in our journey of life. Māori philosophy also emphasizes the profound relationship between humans and nature, encapsulated in the concept of kaitiakitanga, or guardianship.

This belief holds that humans are intrinsically linked to the natural world, which is viewed as an extension of the self. The land (whenua), forests, rivers, and seas are all seen as kin or genealogical connection, deserving of respect and care. This deep bond fosters a sense of responsibility to protect and sustain the environment for future generations.

By recognizing the natural world as an integral part of their identity, Māori people cultivate a holistic sense of self that encompasses both their physical and spiritual connections to the natural environment. This unity with nature not only reinforces their identity but also installs values of stewardship, respect, and harmony with the earth. Through kaitiakitanga, we learn that our identity is not separate from the environment but is enriched and defined by our relationship with it. For those without a cultural background in kaitiakitanga, adopting this philosophy involves fostering a deep respect and sense of responsibility for the planet, recognizing that our well-being is intertwined with the health of the natural world. By embracing the principles of guardianship and sustainability, individuals can cultivate a holistic sense of identity that honors their connection to nature, enriching their lives and communities.

Self-Reflection Questions:

- How does your cultural background or heritage influence your sense of identity?

- In what ways can you strengthen your connection to the natural world as part of your identity?

Identity

My Journey: Overcoming Limiting Beliefs

Growing up in Masterton, New Zealand, I faced the harsh realities of poverty, with parents who struggled with alcohol and gambling addictions. The constant struggle for belonging and acceptance left me yearning for validation as I entered adulthood. With no positive role models or educated figures in my immediate or extended family, I didn't excel in school and eventually dropped out at the young age of fourteen.

During my teens and early adulthood, my fragile self-esteem couldn't handle teasing, leading me to withdraw into my mind, exhibit aggressive behavior, and I coped with a drug addiction and bottled-up emotions, convinced that there was no promising future for me—that I was unworthy and an embarrassment. Instead of taking responsibility for my life, I blamed the world for my circumstances and focused on my troubled past rather than envisioning a promising future. My journey took a transformative turn when I encountered positive role models outside of my family.

Teachers and mentors believed in me, like (Aunty) Paremo Matthews and her family, whom I silently called my "Savior family," treated me like their own, providing me with a foundation for building my self-worth. Learning about my Māori culture in /school played a significant role in reshaping my identity with this newfound support and cultural understanding.

The Path Ahead

I eventually attained my Bachelor of Arts at twenty-one and a Graduate Diploma in Secondary Teaching at twenty-five. Yet, even at thirty, limiting beliefs still conditioned me to believe I wasn't worthy or capable of achieving anything great.

Understanding and embracing my Māori heritage, coupled with the influence of positive role models, helped me break free from the shackles of my past. Attending NLP and personal development seminars further transformed my limiting beliefs, leading to an increase in my self-worth and self-value. This journey gave me a greater sense of purpose and being future oriented. Overcoming my limiting beliefs was pivotal in realizing that my past did not define my future and that I had the power to shape my destiny.

Your Beliefs

Beliefs are an intrinsic part of our identity, so much so that we will fiercely defend them, even when the evidence and facts go against us. This is why, when your beliefs are challenged or not validated, it can feel like a personal attack or as if you're not being heard.

When you struggle with changing what is important, like improving communication with your spouse to build a more meaningful relationship, it's often because a limiting belief is holding you back.

Identity

A belief is a conviction about what something means, often held without concrete evidence.

The way you experience the world is shaped by your beliefs.

You have countless beliefs, many of which you may not even be aware of. Some of these beliefs can sabotage your happiness and potential.

Your brain functions like a vast warehouse that stores memories and experiences, which in turn influence your beliefs.

Limiting Beliefs

According to ChangingMinds.org, limiting beliefs are those that constrain us in some way. By believing them, we restrict our thoughts, actions, and words. These beliefs often relate to our self-identity, fostering a scarcity mindset rather than one of abundance. They create invisible barriers that prevent us from exploring new opportunities and realizing our full potential. Limiting beliefs are usually rooted in past experiences and negative self-perceptions, reinforcing a cycle of self-doubt and fear.

Limiting beliefs manifest as excuses such as:

"I will never have money because I grew up in a poor family without positive role models for financial success."

"I would have achieved my goals if it weren't for my kids, partner, the pandemic, floods..."

"I can't get over my breakup, so I will never marry again."

"I'll be happy once I'm rich."

"I will never find the love of my life because I end up hurting people."

"I could never be a teacher because I dropped out of school early."

"If my parents had taught me better, I would have..."

Self-Reflection Questions:

- What are some of the limiting beliefs you hold? How have they impacted your life decisions?

- How would your life change if you replaced these limiting beliefs with empowering ones?

Defining Moments

Defining moments are pivotal events in your life that significantly shape your beliefs, values, and perceptions of yourself and the world. These moments often serve as critical turning points that influence your decisions and the direction of your personal journey. As children, we are not responsible for what happens to us, but as adults, we are responsible for how we respond to our past.

Identity

Blaming our current circumstances on our childhood is unproductive and only serves to hold us back. According to Tony Robbins, "It's not what happens to you, but how you react to it that matters."

Clinging to past traumas and assigning blame for our adult status on our childhood limits our potential, stunts our growth, and fosters fear. This fear, in turn, perpetuates limiting beliefs that shape a dysfunctional mindset. The individuals who are central to our lives during childhood—parents, caregivers, teachers, and peers—play a significant role in shaping our self-beliefs and the internal dialogue we maintain. These early interactions and experiences are crucial to our development and influence our perspective of the world.

Both pleasant and unpleasant moments from our childhood help to define us and condition our ways of thinking, shaping our beliefs, and forming the foundation for our values.

When we are young, and someone close to us—whether a parent, friend, or sibling hurts us, our primary response is simply, "That hurt!" Without the maturity or awareness to understand the context, we often internalize these experiences, associating them with guilt or self-blame. As children, we lack the insight to recognize that another person's poor choices are not a reflection of our worth. Consequently, many of us carry forward anger, resentment, regret, self-pity, or blame attached to these formative memories.

Due to a natural human tendency known as "negativity bias," we are more likely to remember negative experiences from our past than positive ones. Sometimes, we may not even recall certain events because we were too young to remember, or our minds have suppressed these memories for protection.

Self-Reflection Questions:

- Reflect on a defining moment from your past. How has it shaped your beliefs and values today?

- What positive lessons can you take from that experience to empower your future?

Breaking Free From Limiting Beliefs: a 5-step guide

Breaking free from limiting beliefs is crucial for personal growth. Here's a five-step guide, inspired by experts in the industry, to help you overcome these mental barriers and unlock your true potential:

1. **Identify Limiting Beliefs**

   o **Spot the Culprits**: Start by recognizing the thoughts that hold you back, like "I'm not good enough" or "I don't deserve success."

   o **Take Action**: Jot down these beliefs. Reflect on their origins— what past experiences or influences shaped these thoughts?

2. **Challenge and Question Your Beliefs**

   o **Put Them on Trial**: Scrutinize your limiting beliefs. Are they really true, or just perceptions you've built over time?

   o **Take Action**: For each belief, ask yourself, "Is this really true?" and "What evidence do I have that contradicts this belief?" Find counter examples that prove these beliefs wrong.

3. **Replace Negative Beliefs With Empowering Ones**

   o **Flip the Script**: Turn your negative beliefs into positive affirmations that reflect your true potential.

   o **Take Action**: Transform "I can't do this" into "I am capable, and I can find a way." Write down these empowering beliefs and repeat them daily.

4. **Take Action Towards Your Goals**

   o **Break the Cycle**: Taking concrete steps towards your goals helps reinforce new, positive beliefs.

   o **Take Action**: Set small, achievable goals aligned with your new beliefs. Celebrate every success, no matter how small, to boost your confidence.

5. **Surround Yourself with Positive Influences**

   o **Build a Support Network**: Engage with people and environments that support your growth and reinforce your beliefs.

   o **Take Action**: Find mentors, join supportive groups, and steer clear of negative influences. Immerse yourself in positive, encouraging environments.

   o

By identifying and challenging your limiting beliefs, replacing them with empowering ones, taking action, and surrounding yourself with positive influences, you can transform your mindset and achieve your goals. Remember, awareness, critical questioning, and consistent positive action are key to overcoming the barriers that hold you back.

Your Values

Around the age of ten, we begin to develop our values and opinions about the world. These values shape our perspective and how we cope with life's challenges. Values are the emotional states you want to experience consistently, such as joy, love, compassion, understanding, or, conversely, misery, resentment, and anger. Therefore, it's crucial to have a clear understanding of the values we are unconsciously unaware of.

Identity

Have you ever found it difficult to decide on something? Often, this is because you are unclear about what you value most in that situation. When something doesn't feel right, it's likely because it conflicts with your core values.

Conflicts and annoyances often arise from differing values between people. In relationships, it's not necessary for both partners to have identical values; diversity in values can strengthen a relationship by bringing different perspectives and strengths. The secret to enduring happiness, even during tough times, is to live congruently with your values. When you know what's most important to you, making decisions and plans becomes straightforward. Living in alignment with your values provides a foundation for adventure, achievement, and growth.

When you are clear about your values, you understand what you stand for, which drives your decisions and actions. Your values serve as an internal compass, aligning you with your true self and providing assurance when making decisions.

They either propel you towards your goals or hold you back, and being aware of this empowers you to live life on your terms. As Stephen R. Covey, author of *The 7 Habits of Highly Effective People*, states, "Your values determine your decisions and priorities in life."

Values;

define who you are and who you aspire to be.

guide your decisions and actions, acting as a moral compass.

influence your happiness and fulfillment, depending on what you prioritize.

drive and motivate you, ensuring that even in challenging times, you act in alignment with your principles.

shape your beliefs and have consequences based on their prioritization.

Your lifestyle reflects the standards of your values.

Self-Reflection Questions:

What are your current values? How do they align with the life you want to live?

Are there any values you need to adjust or adopt to better align with your goals?

Building Pleasure and Purpose

The categorization of "Hedonistic" and "Meaning" values is a simplified yet powerful way to understand the different motivations and priorities driving your behaviour. "Hedonistic" values focus on seeking pleasure and immediate gratification, while "Meaning" values emphasize long-term fulfillment and purpose. Mastering the art of choosing meaningful values often involves enduring short-term discomfort for long-term benefits, sacrificing instant gratification for future rewards. While this categorization is useful, it's important to recognize that values can be more complex and nuanced. Different psychological theories and models may categorize values differently, highlighting the intricate nature of human motivation. By exploring and balancing both hedonistic and meaningful values, you can build a life rich in both pleasure and purpose.

Hedonistic Values are focused on the pursuit of pleasure, enjoyment, and immediate gratification. They prioritize personal happiness, sensory pleasure, and the avoidance of pain or discomfort.

Focus on immediate gratification and comfort.

Driven by a desire for pleasure in the present.

Example: "I want it now."

Meaning Values are centred around purpose, significance, and fulfillment. They prioritize long-term goals, contributions to society, and the achievement of personal growth and self-actualization.

Focus on long-term goals and meaningful outcomes.

Require patience and delayed gratification.

Example: Sacrificing immediate comfort for future success.

Aligning Your Core Values

Tip #1: To discover what you value most, reflect on where you spend most of your time and money. Are you happy with the feelings associated with these priorities?

Tip #2: Remember, you have the power to choose your values at any moment. Choose values like passion, love, determination, and discipline over emotions like anger, misery, sadness, guilt, and blame.

Tip #3: Identify your goals or purpose. What values will you need to achieve these goals? List these values and rank them from 1 to 5, where 5 indicates the highest focus and commitment.

Activity: What Are Your Current Values? Take a moment to reflect on where you spend most of your money and time. These choices often reveal your true values.

1. **Permission to Reflect**: Give yourself permission to be honest with what you discover as you list your values. There may be some values that align perfectly with what you want and others that conflict. Recognizing these discrepancies is a crucial step in aligning your life with your true desires.

2. **Core Feelings and Emotional States**: Identify the core feelings or emotional states you need to experience daily, such as joy, playfulness, happiness, creativity, energy, fun, and compassion. When you consciously cultivate these emotions, you remain true to yourself and create a more fulfilling life.

3. **Reflect on Past Experiences**: Recall a time when you genuinely felt these emotions. What were you doing? Who were you with? Understanding these moments can help you identify activities and relationships that nurture your authentic self.

4. **Rules Around Your Values**: Consider the personal rules or standards that govern your values. For example, one of my core values is love. To live by this value, I remind myself to infuse love into everything I do. If I find myself getting angry, I pause and ask, "What would love do in this situation?" Another personal rule I have is to value respect in all my communications with others.

"What the mind believes the body conceives." - *Napoleon Hill*

Building Belief and Worth With Self-Affirmations

Using self-affirmations regularly is a powerful way to enhance your self-esteem. People who consistently use self-affirmations often find that they perform better and take greater pride in their actions. Self-affirmations are essential building blocks for self-esteem.

The Path Ahead

As Brian Tracy, a renowned motivational speaker, says, *"The person we believe ourselves to be will always act in a manner consistent with our self-image."* People with high self-esteem, without falling into egoism, habitually achieve their goals, have a clear direction in life, and are willing to make mistakes to grow.

In 2018, I found myself in a challenging mental space, stuck in a rut that brought on a lack of motivation and a level of depression. I realized that only I could encourage and trust myself to overcome this adversity. One of my daily morning rituals became verbalizing self-affirmations in front of a mirror. Although I didn't initially believe much of what I affirmed to myself, I had no choice but to trust in the process. This practice, which allowed me to plant and nurture a seed of belief, became a powerful initiation.

After about five months, I started to genuinely believe in the affirmations I repeated, and my body began to feel self-trust and courage, giving me a sense of security and the belief that I would be okay. Now, a glance at my reflection or when I see videos and photos of myself triggers pride, gratification, and confidence. This ritual significantly improved my positive self-talk and boosted my confidence to take risks. Affirmations such as "I am an amazing person," "I am loved," and "I am important to others" played a crucial role in transforming my mindset.

Adopting Positive Affirmations

What are five affirmations or types of beliefs you can adopt today to serve you well? Here are some examples:

- "I have a lot to give to others."

- "I am willing to try new things."

- "I trust myself to follow through on what I say."

- "I have all I need within me right now."

- "I can accomplish anything I set my mind to."

- "I am confident and strong."

Take a moment to write down five affirmations that resonate with you. Use the space below to jot them down and reflect on how they can help shift your mindset:

1. _____

2. _____

3. _____

4. _____

5. _____

Conclusion As you reflect on the importance of understanding your values and aligning your actions with your authentic self, consider the barriers that might hold you back from living in full alignment with who you truly are. Often, these barriers are rooted in fear of judgment, fear of failure, or fear of the unknown. But what if you could transcend these fears and step into a life driven by courage instead of hesitation? Imagine how your life would change if you weren't held back by the fear of what others might think or the possibility of making mistakes.

As we close this chapter, let's prepare to delve into the nature of fear, exploring how it affects our decisions, limits our potential, and, more importantly, how we can confront and overcome it. The next chapter will guide you on a journey of living courageously—where facing your fears becomes the key to unlocking the life you've always dreamed of. Let's move forward with the courage to embrace vulnerability, take action, and live authentically.

CHAPTER FOUR

Fear

Breaking the Chains

"The primary cause of unhappiness is never the situation but your thoughts about it." - Eckhart Tolle

Living Courageously

1. Imagine living your life without worrying about what others think of you. How would that change your world?

2. What if you overcame the fear of failure and started doing the things you've held back on for so long?

3. How would that benefit you and those around you?

Holding onto fear or delaying decisions is like sitting on a metaphorical fence. The longer you sit there, the more the discomfort grows, the fear strengthens, and your confidence diminishes. Think about how many opportunities you've missed because fear stood in your way.

If you're serious about making changes in your life, you'll need to face your fears head-on. Facing fear and taking action despite it requires both a decision and courage, which can unlock incredible opportunities.

When you step into fear, you begin living the life you've always envisioned and doing the things you enjoy doing, doing what you love. By embracing fear, you also acknowledge and accept vulnerability. When we are open to vulnerability, we invite authenticity into our lives. This fosters deeper connections with others and strengthens relationships. Showing your true self, including your fears and insecurities, creates an environment of trust and mutual understanding.

Remember, courage isn't the absence of fear but the willingness to move forward despite it. When you embrace your fears, not only do you grow as an individual, but you also inspire others to confront their own fears.

Beyond Fear: Unlocking Potential Through Action

Waiting for fear to disappear is futile, courage comes from action. Taking action builds resilience and uncovers inner strength. Growth and change often involve discomfort, but they open the door to greater opportunities, adventure, and willingness to take risks. Take a moment to reflect on a time when you were too scared to act and later regretted it. What opportunities did you miss by letting fear control you?

Now think of a time when you faced your fears and later wished you had done it sooner. What did you feel afterward—relief, progress, or achievement? Reflecting on these moments can remind you of the control and potential you must shape in your life.

When we familiarize ourselves with our fears and embrace uncertainty, we become more willing to take risks and step out of our comfort zones. By shedding the fear of judgment, we aim higher and take bolder actions. Staying in our comfort zone means nothing changes, leaving us with lingering "what ifs." Facing fears can also inspire others and show them what is possible on their journeys.

Reflection Exercise:

Think of a recent situation where fear held you back. What would have changed if you had taken action? Write down three benefits you would have gained from confronting that fear.

1.

2.

3.

Now, write one small step you can take this week toward facing a similar fear.

One Step:

Where Does Fear Come From?

Fear is triggered by a small part of the brain called the amygdala, responsible for our fight-or-flight responses. This survival mechanism has been with us since ancient times when our ancestors relied on it to avoid dangers in their environment. Today, fear manifests in modern contexts—such as public speaking, financial stress, or social interactions. These situations may not be life-threatening, but they still activate our brain's protective instincts, often keeping us in our comfort zones.

Fear is a natural and universal emotion that serves as a survival tool, but it can also limit us when it arises from less tangible sources like anxiety, past traumas, or societal pressures. Cultural norms can instil fears of failure, rejection, or not fitting in. Understanding these psychological roots of fear allows us to challenge them. By recognizing the narratives we tell ourselves and re-examining them, we can transform fear from a force that paralyzes us into one that motivates growth. The amygdala's role in keeping us safe is essential, but unchecked, it can prevent us from fully appreciating our lives and achieving our dreams. While fear can save us from danger, it can also inhibit our potential.

Levels of Fear: From Survival to Self-Actualization

I remember one time having a conversation with someone who was in the middle of their personal growth journey who mentioned to me that there was no such thing as fear.

Fear

As much as I knew they were coming from a place of getting over fear and facing it anyway, I still needed to explain to him my understanding of fear.

This is where the three levels of fear comes into introduction. In her book *Your Success: 10 Steps to an Extraordinary Life*, Sharon Pearson categorizes fear into three levels:

1. **Level One: Realistic Fears**
   - Death, being alone, accidents, growing old, losing a loved one, illness.

2. **Level Two: Action-Required Fears**
   - Public speaking, intimacy, making friends, ending toxic relationships, asking someone out, losing weight.

3. **Level Three: Inner-State Fears**
   - Rejection, judgment, vulnerability, success, failure, disapproval, and exposure.

At the root of all fears are three core beliefs:

- I am not good enough.

- I don't belong.

- I am not loved.

These fears influence many of our decisions, from relationships to career choices.

For example, if you're afraid to ask someone out, it's not just the fear of rejection but the fear of being perceived as "not good enough." When we allow these beliefs to dominate, they prevent us from fully experiencing life.

Case Story: Michael Embraces Vulnerability and Builds Stronger Connections

Consider Michael, a successful business executive with a seemingly perfect life— thriving career, beautiful home, and a loving family. However, behind the scenes, his marriage is struggling. He fears opening up emotionally to his wife, believing she might see him as weak. His fear of vulnerability also distances him from his children, creating emotional barriers.

At work, Michael micromanages his team because he's afraid they won't complete tasks to his standards. His fear of failure stops him from pursuing a new business venture he is passionate about, as he worries about judgment if it doesn't succeed.

By recognizing his fears and understanding their roots, Michael begins to change. He has honest conversations with his wife, which strengthens their connection.

He engages more with his children, showing genuine interest in their lives. At work, he learns to delegate, trust his team, and take steps toward his business venture. As a result, Michael transforms his personal and professional life, proving that facing fear can lead to profound positive changes.

Cultivating a Healthy Relationship With Fear

Developing a healthy relationship with fear involves acceptance and proactive management. Techniques like mindfulness, meditation, and deep-breathing exercises help you stay grounded when fear arises. These practices encourage you to observe your fear without judgment, giving you the space to respond thoughtfully rather than react impulsively.

In *The Power of Now*, Eckhart Tolle addresses the importance of focusing on the present moment to overcome fear. Tolle explains that fear often stems from our identification with the ego and its attachment to future anxieties. When we practice mindfulness and focus on the present, we diminish the power of fear. By staying grounded, we regain control and weaken fear's grip on our lives.

Practical Tool: Mindful Breathing

When fear arises, take three slow, deep breaths, focusing your attention solely on your breath. This simple act brings your awareness to the present moment and helps ease anxiety. Practice this regularly to build resilience.

Practical Tool: Reframe Your Thoughts

Next time fear arises, reframe your thinking from "What if I fail?" to "What can I learn from this?" Shifting your focus to growth opportunities turns fear into a stepping stone for success.

The Path Ahead

Daily Practices to Build Resilience

Building resilience is a daily practice. Eleanor Roosevelt once said, "Do one thing every day that scares you." This philosophy encourages us to step out of our comfort zones and confront fears head-on, building mental and emotional strength.

For the past few years, I've adopted this philosophy. In 2024, my goal was to publish this book, confronting my fear of judgment. In 2023, I resigned from my corporate job to build my life coaching business, facing the fear of financial instability. In 2022, I tackled my insecurities in fitness settings by regularly attending the gym. Each year, I have embraced a specific fear, which has ultimately led to personal growth.

Daily practices like cold showers or public speaking in small groups help build resilience to discomfort. Gradually increasing exposure to fear-inducing situations strengthens your ability to manage stress and handle challenges effectively.

Practical Tool: Daily Exposure

Write down one fear you have. Commit to doing one small thing every day that edges you closer to confronting it. Over time, you'll build the resilience and confidence needed to face it fully.

Conclusion

Throughout this chapter, we've explored how fear impacts us and how embracing it can unlock tremendous growth. By understanding the biological and psychological roots of fear and practicing daily resilience-building activities, you can transform fear into a powerful tool for self-improvement. Fear is a natural part of life, but it doesn't have to limit you. By facing your fears, you unlock your true potential and inspire others to do the same.

As we move forward, the next chapter will explore the concept of character; the core standards and traits that guide you through life's challenges. Facing fear builds resilience, but it is your character that shapes your decisions. Together, let's continue this journey of self-discovery and step boldly into the adventure of self-mastery

CHAPTER FIVE

Character

Building The Foundation

"Character is the real foundation of all worthwhile success"

- John Hays Hammond

Character is The Real Foundation

Imagine standing at the crossroads of your life, where every choice you make builds upon the last, laying the bricks of your future. At this pivotal moment, what will guide your decisions? What will keep you steadfast when the winds of adversity blow? The answer lies in your character. Character isn't just a trait of the successful or the famous; it's the bedrock upon which all meaningful and lasting achievements are built. It's not about the success that others see, but the quiet, steadfast qualities that shape who you are at your core. Whether you're striving to build a business, overcome personal challenges, or maintain strong relationships, character is what will see you through.

Character

In this chapter, we'll explore how cultivating a strong character is essential for achieving the life you truly want. You'll learn how daily habits shape your identity and how the principles and practices of highly effective individuals can help you forge a character that not only withstands challenges but thrives in the face of adversity.

Consider the stories of Bob Marley, Michael Jordan, Steve Jobs, and others who started with nothing more than their inner drive. What sets these individuals apart? It's not just talent or luck—it's character. They didn't merely dream of success; they hammered and forged their character, day by day, decision by decision, until it became the foundation of their achievements.

In *How to Win Friends and Influence People*, Dale Carnegie teaches that our character and self-perception are the keys to influencing others and achieving success. He reminds us that it's not what we do occasionally that shapes our character, but what we do consistently. The leaders who inspire, the individuals who achieve, all share this common thread: a strong, positive self-belief, clarity of purpose, and unwavering commitment to their values. As we delve into this chapter, you'll discover that character is more than just a set of traits, it's the essence of who you are becoming. And in that becoming lies the power to achieve your greatest aspirations and connect deeply with others.

Cultivating Character Through Personal Development

Personal development is the crucible in which character is forged. It's the process that allows you to grow year after year, improving not only yourself but also positively impacting those you love. True personal development goes beyond enhancing your mindset; it involves nurturing every aspect of your being—your health, your relationships, and your sense of purpose.Jim Rohn famously said, *"Success is something you attract by the person you become."* When you focus on personal development, you begin to attract success naturally, not because of what you have, but because of who you are becoming. It's about continually refining your skills, your mindset, and every facet of your life to build a character that is resilient, adaptable, and capable of overcoming any challenge.

A well-developed character not only helps you navigate life's difficulties but also positions you as a person of influence. You become someone who others look up to, trust, and want to be around. This doesn't happen overnight, but through a commitment to daily habits that align with the person you aspire to be.

Embracing Adversity as a Catalyst For Growth

It's often through facing adversity that we discover our true strengths and develop the qualities that define our character. Whether it's the loss of a job, a personal failure, or a difficult relationship, these challenges teach us resilience, patience, and the power of perseverance. Consider how some of the most admired figures in history—like Nelson Mandela, J.K. Rowling, and Abraham Lincoln—faced enormous challenges and emerged stronger, with characters forged in the fires of adversity. These experiences remind us that setbacks are not the end but rather the beginning of a new chapter in our development.

As you cultivate your character, you'll notice a shift in your life. You'll start attracting a community of like-minded individuals who share your values and aspirations. The world will begin to look different as you change your perspective, seeing opportunities where you once saw obstacles. This transformation is inevitable once you change the way you see yourself and the world around you.

In Legacy by James Kerr, which explores the success of the New Zealand All Blacks rugby team, character is identified as a critical component of their unparalleled achievements. The team doesn't just focus on skill; they prioritize character building. One of their core principles is "Sweep the Shed," which means that no matter what the outcome of the game, players clean their locker rooms, reinforcing humility and responsibility. This simple act speaks volumes about their character. It's about doing what's right, not just when the world is watching, but in every moment, big or small.

Cultivating Character Through Self-reflection

Building character isn't just about what you do; it's also about how you think. Regular self-reflection is a powerful tool for growth, allowing you to assess your actions, learn from your experiences, and ensure that your behaviors are aligned with your core values. Consider setting aside time each day or week to reflect on questions such as: "What did I learn today?" "How did I handle challenges?" "What areas of my character need further development?"

The Path Ahead

By making self-reflection a habit, you can continually refine your character, ensuring that it evolves alongside your personal and professional growth.

Shaping Character Through Your Environment

The environment you choose to surround yourself with plays a significant role in shaping your character. The people you interact with, the spaces you occupy, and the influences you allow into your life all contribute to the person you become. Surround yourself with individuals who inspire you, challenge you to grow, and reflect the values you aspire to embody. Create spaces that foster focus, creativity, and well-being. Just as a plant thrives in the right environment, so too will your character flourish when nurtured in a supportive and enriching setting.

Building Character Three Essential Steps.
1. Compliment Others Often

Complimenting others is one of the simplest yet most powerful ways to build character. It shifts your focus from criticism to appreciation, fostering a more positive outlook on life and relationships. When you interact with others, make it a habit to notice something you genuinely admire. Whether it's a colleague's work ethic, a friend's kindness, or a stranger's warm smile, express your appreciation.

Start small: when you buy something at a shop, thank the person serving you with a specific compliment. For example, "I really appreciate your bright smile; it made my day." Aim to compliment at least five people each day. This habit not only brightens others' days but also cultivates a spirit of gratitude within you.

Receiving compliments is equally important. If you struggle with accepting praise, make a conscious effort to embrace it. When someone compliments you, don't deflect it; simply say, "Thank you." This practice will strengthen your self-esteem and reinforce your self-worth.

2. Model Excellence

Excellence isn't about perfection; it's about striving to be the best version of yourself. To model excellence, study the lives of those who have achieved the success you aspire to. Explore their habits, their mindset, and the principles that guide them.

Look at historical figures, contemporary leaders, or even mentors in your own life. What do they do daily that sets them apart? How do they handle challenges? Do they have rituals or routines that ground them? By understanding what makes these individuals successful, you can adopt and adapt those qualities to fit your own journey. Remember, you don't have to mimic anyone entirely. Take what resonates with you and integrate those practices into your life. Excellence is about continuous improvement and commitment to growth.

3. Build Your Self-Trust

Self-trust is the cornerstone of a strong character. It's the belief that you can rely on yourself to make decisions, handle challenges, and stay true to your values. Building self-trust starts with small, consistent actions that reinforce your confidence in your abilities. Establish daily rituals that you commit to, no matter the circumstances. These could be as simple as making your bed every morning, walking 6,000-10,000 steps daily, or spending 20 minutes in meditation.

The Path Ahead

Each time you honor these commitments; you strengthen your trust in yourself. Over time, as you build self-trust, you'll find it easier to step out of your comfort zone and take on bigger challenges. You'll begin to trust not only yourself but also the process, knowing that each step forward, no matter how small, is a victory in itself.

Create Your Rituals

Rituals are the bedrock of character building. In his book *The Power of Habit*, Charles Duhigg explains how habits shape our lives and how establishing positive routines can lead to significant improvements in various areas. James Clear, in *Atomic Habits*, reinforces this idea, highlighting the transformative power of small, consistent actions. Daily rituals empower you to face challenges with resilience and purpose. They boost your well-being, foster a sense of achievement, and keep you aligned with your long-term goals. Start with simple rituals, such as walking daily, making your bed, or journaling in the mornings. These small actions, repeated consistently, create a foundation of discipline and focus.

Here are some ritual ideas to consider:

- **Walk 6,000-10,000 Steps Daily**: A manageable goal that promotes physical health and builds trust in your ability to meet daily targets.

- **Make Your Bed Every Morning**: A practice that cultivates discipline and sets a positive tone for the day.

- **Take Cold Showers**: Benefits include increased blood flow and resilience-building stress

- **Sweep the Floor Daily**: This simple task keeps your environment and mindset in order.

- **20-Minute Workout**: Boosts dopamine levels and improves physical health.

- **Journal in the Mornings**: Reflect on your thoughts and emotions to process them healthily.

- **Spend 20 Minutes in Silence**: Use this time for mindfulness, such as watching the sunrise or sunset.

- **Learn Something New Daily**: Keep your mind sharp by dedicating time to reading or studying.

- **Disconnect Before Bed**: Avoid electronics two hours before sleep to reflect on your day and prepare for restful sleep.

These rituals are more than just tasks; they are daily affirmations of your commitment to personal growth. By integrating them into your life, you build a character that is strong, resilient, and aligned with your highest aspirations.

Rising Above: From School Drop Out to Performing Arts Achiever

When I was 17, I attended Whitireia Performing Arts in Porirua, New Zealand—a pivotal moment in my life. There, I learned more than just performing, dancing, and entertaining; I gained life skills that would shape my future roles as an Assistant Cruise Director, Tour Guide, and Life Coach. At Whitireia, we were held to the highest standards of excellence. After every performance, we would gather as a team to debrief, receiving feedback that was both constructive and challenging. This wasn't just about refining our craft; it was about building character.

The Path Ahead

Traveling the world with Whitireia was an experience I never imagined growing up. As a child, I often went without. I was always one of the last in the class to purchase my school stationery and school uniform while I often had no lunch at school, so the idea of overseas travel was beyond my wildest dreams. Yet there I was, performing in ancient castles in France, singing in bullfighting arenas in Spain, and dancing for Pope John Paul II in Vatican City. These experiences taught me the power of perseverance, discipline, and the importance of building a strong character. The feedback we received after each performance was a gift. It was through this rigorous process of self-assessment and improvement that I learned the importance of constantly striving to be better. This is a lesson that applies to all areas of life—we must always be willing to learn, grow, and push beyond our comfort zones.

Left to right:
St. Peter's Square, Vatican City, Rome, 1998 – We attended mass and performed for Pope John Paul II.
Front page of *La Escalerona,* **Gijón, Spain, 1999 –** I was interviewed about my impressions of Spain and how it compared to New Zealand.
Battery Park, New York City, 1997 – With the Twin Towers in the background, we had attended folklore festival in Waynesville, North Carolina.

Self-reflection Questions

Future Pacing: If you we were to go five, ten, fifteen years into the future what would that look like to you? If you have all the resources and no limitations holding you back, and you were able to create your ideal future what would you see, hear, and notice about that picture?

> ➤ What are you doing?
> ➤ What can you do?
> ➤ How are you feeling?

Who are you being in that moment in time? *Notice the success you have, the sensational feelings you may be experiencing.*

> ➤ What were the attributes you would have acquired for you to get to that future place?
> ➤ How many of these attributes do you demonstrate daily today?
> ➤ What attributes will you need to change and start to develop?

Conclusion As you move forward, remember that character is not built in a day, but through the choices you make daily. Every action, every decision, and every challenge faced with integrity and courage adds a brick to the foundation of who you are becoming. Embrace the journey of building your character, knowing that it is the key to unlocking the life you truly desire.

The Path Ahead

You have the power to shape your destiny—one act of character at a time. In the next chapter, we will delve into the impact of trauma and how it intersects with your journey of self-discovery. Understanding and healing from trauma is essential in fully embracing who you are and continuing to build the character that shapes your life. Together, let's explore how acknowledging and working through past wounds can empower you to move forward with even greater strength and resilience.

CHAPTER SIX

Trauma

From Darkness to Light

"Heal the boy and the man will appear" - Tony Robbins

Unveiling Trauma

In this chapter, we will explore the nature of trauma. We will look at how it affects both your mental and physical health, and why it is essential to engage in the healing process. By viewing trauma through a lens of understanding and compassion, we can begin to dismantle the barriers it creates, paving the way for personal growth and well-being. Healing from trauma is not just about overcoming past pain; it is about reclaiming your life, enhancing your resilience, and fostering a deeper connection with yourself and others. Trauma can be an invisible force that profoundly shapes our lives, often without our conscious awareness.

It may manifest through various symptoms such as anxiety, depression, relationship difficulties, and even physical ailments. Trauma's impact is not limited to those who have experienced catastrophic events; it can affect anyone who has faced significant stress or emotional pain.

Understanding how trauma influences your life is crucial because it enables you to address the underlying issues that may be holding you back from achieving your full potential.

As a leader, you recognize the importance of effective communication and leadership. However, unresolved trauma can undermine these skills at home. It may lead to impatience with your spouse, frustration toward your children, and difficulty connecting on an emotional level. Recognizing and addressing these issues is essential for fostering a loving and supportive family environment.

Understanding Trauma: Big T and Small t

The term "formative years" refers to the early period in a person's life, typically from birth to around age eight, when significant physical, emotional, social, and cognitive development takes place. During these years, experiences and interactions with caregivers, peers, and the environment play a crucial role in shaping an individual's personality, beliefs, behaviors, and overall development. These foundational experiences can have long-lasting impacts on a person's future well-being and relationships.

Trauma

Gabor Maté, a Canadian physician and author specializing in childhood development and trauma, explains that "Trauma is a psychic wound that hardens you psychologically, interfering with your ability to grow and develop. It pains you, causing you to act out of pain. It induces fear, leading you to act out of fear." He emphasizes that "trauma is not what happens to you; it's what happens inside you because of what happened to you."

Gabor Maté differentiates between "Big T" trauma and "Small t" trauma to explain the various ways trauma can manifest in a person's life. This distinction helps in understanding that trauma is not limited to catastrophic events but includes more subtle, everyday experiences that can still have significant psychological impacts.

Big T Trauma

Big T Trauma refers to major, life-altering events that are typically severe and shocking. These types of traumas are widely recognized and can include:

- **Natural Disasters:** Experiencing or witnessing earthquakes, hurricanes, floods, etc.
- **War and Violence:** Being involved in combat, terrorist attacks, or violent crime.
- **Severe Accidents:** Car crashes, industrial accidents, or other life-threatening incidents.

- **Physical or Sexual Abuse:** Any form of significant physical harm or sexual violation.

These traumas can happen at any age.

An often-overlooked factor is the environment and the emotions a child is exposed to. A child can pick up on the emotions of their parents and the energy around them. For example, a parent who experiences anxiety will demonstrate certain traits and behaviors that the child can sense.

Other examples of trauma in childhood include:

- **Domestic Violence:** Experiencing or witnessing domestic violence, which involves repeated exposure to physical, emotional, or psychological abuse, deeply affects an individual's sense of safety and self-worth.

- **A Parent Who Is Mentally Ill:** Growing up with a parent who has a severe mental illness can be extremely traumatic, particularly if it affects the parent's ability to provide stable, nurturing care. This can lead to feelings of neglect, fear, and insecurity in the child.

- **A Parent with Addictive Behaviors:** Having a parent who struggles with addiction can create a chaotic and unsafe home environment. The unpredictability and potential for neglect or abuse in these situations can be highly traumatic for children.

- **Poverty:** While not always classified under Big T trauma, severe poverty can be traumatic, especially if it leads to chronic stress, lack of basic needs, exposure to crime, or homelessness. The constant struggle for survival can have long-lasting psychological effects.
- **Extreme Inequality/Racism:** Experiences of severe inequality or racism can be traumatic, especially when they involve violence, systemic discrimination, or persistent societal exclusion. These experiences can lead to a deep sense of fear, injustice, and psychological harm.

These events are often associated with a high risk of developing Post-Traumatic Stress Disorder (PTSD) and other severe mental health issues. Big T trauma can leave deep psychological scars that require intensive healing processes.

Small t Trauma

Small t Trauma involves less intense but more chronic or cumulative experiences that still cause emotional harm. These may include:

- **Emotional Neglect:** Growing up in an environment where emotional needs are not met.
- **Bullying:** Repeated harassment or intimidation, especially during formative years.

- **Divorce or Relationship Issues:** The emotional turmoil from parental divorce or problematic relationships.

- **Chronic Stress:** Persistent stressors like ongoing financial struggles, job instability, or long-term illness.

While these experiences might not be as immediately shocking or severe as Big T traumas, they can still profoundly affect an individual's mental health, self-esteem, and emotional stability over time. Small t trauma can lead to chronic anxiety, depression, and other emotional challenges. Children can be wounded even in a loving family when their emotional and physical needs are not fully met. The need to be loved unconditionally, picked up when distressed, and soothed promptly is crucial for their emotional development.

Being left to cry for too long without attention can cause significant stress. Similarly, witnessing inappropriate situations, such as parents arguing or engaging in intimate acts, can also be traumatic. Gabor Maté emphasizes the importance of loving your child unconditionally, applying affectionate touch, and demonstrating expressions of love during the first three years of life. When these needs are not met, it creates emotional wounds that can manifest in various ways later in life. Another form of Small 't' trauma can occur right from birth. For example, a smack on the bum by a midwife to check if a child is breathing, or other stressful events surrounding childbirth, can be traumatic for some individuals.

Identifying Your Own Traumas

Can you identify any Small 't' or Big 'T' traumas from your past that might still be affecting your mental health and relationships today?

Reflecting on past experiences with curiosity and compassion can help uncover hidden wounds that may still influence your thoughts, emotions, and behaviors today. Recognizing these patterns is the first step toward healing and reclaiming your sense of self.

Here's a fictional example designed to illustrate the concept of Small t trauma in childhood:

Emily grew up in a loving family where her parents provided for her physical needs and ensured she had a stable home. However, despite their best intentions, Emily's emotional needs were often unmet.

As a baby, Emily frequently cried for long periods without being comforted, as her parents believed in letting her "self-soothe." They were unaware that this approach could cause her significant stress and anxiety.

As she grew older, Emily was exposed to situations that, while not overtly harmful, left lasting emotional scars. For example, there were times when she overheard her parents arguing intensely, leaving her feeling scared and insecure.

Additionally, once when she was very young, she accidentally walked in on her parents during an intimate moment. Although her parents quickly reassured her, the confusion and discomfort of that experience lingered.

Despite the overall loving environment, these small, seemingly minor experiences accumulated and impacted Emily's emotional development. She began to internalize feelings of being neglected and misunderstood. Emily's need for unconditional love and

As an adult, Emily struggled with forming close relationships. She often felt anxious and insecure, fearing abandonment and rejection.

The emotional wounds from her childhood made her overly sensitive to perceived slights or neglect, impacting her personal and professional relationships.

Understanding the distinction between Big 'T' and Small 't' trauma is crucial because it broadens the scope of what is considered traumatic. This awareness allows individuals to recognize and validate ther experiences of trauma, even if they do not fit the conventional image of a traumatic event. It also underscores the importance of addressing all forms of trauma in the healing process.

Inner Work with Healing and Personal Development

In the context of healing, inner work involves addressing past traumas, emotional wounds, and psychological pain. This process requires introspection, self-compassion, and techniques like therapy, meditation, breathwork, journaling, and mindfulness to heal unresolved issues. Healing inner work focuses on understanding and resolving the root causes of emotional and psychological distress, which can lead to improved mental health and emotional balance.

In the realm of personal development, inner work is about self-discovery, self-improvement, and achieving one's full potential. It includes setting goals, developing new skills, enhancing self-awareness, and cultivating healthy habits and attitudes.

This inner work fosters personal growth, improves relationships, and enhances success in life. Healing and personal development often overlap; healing past traumas removes barriers to growth, while personal development fosters self-worth, aiding healing. Both involve deep self-exploration creating a balanced, fulfilled, and resilient individual.

Psychedelics and Plant Medicine in Healing

As we look more into the realm of healing, it's essential to explore the expanding interest in alternative healing modalities, particularly the use of psychedelics and plant medicines.

In recent years psilocybin mushrooms, and ayahuasca have gained attention for their potential to heal deep-seated trauma and promote psychological well-being. These substances, which have been used for centuries in various indigenous cultures, are now being studied scientifically for their ability to facilitate profound personal insights and emotional healing.

DMT and Ayahuasca

DMT is a powerful psychedelic compound found in certain plants and animals. When consumed in its natural form as part of the ayahuasca brew, DMT induces intense, visionary experiences that can reveal deep emotional and psychological insights.

Ayahuasca ceremonies, traditionally conducted by shamans, are spiritual rituals designed to help participants connect with their subconscious, confront their fears, and gain a greater understanding of their life's purpose. Having personally participated in several ayahuasca retreats, I have experienced firsthand the profound and transformative power of this plant medicine.

These ceremonies have provided me and many of my close friends with a deeper understanding of ourselves and the world around us, both in the seen and unseen realms. My connection to nature has deepened, allowing me to appreciate its beauty and wisdom in ways I never imagined. The ability to sit in silence, once a challenge, has become an expansive and mindful practice, enabling me to connect more deeply with my thoughts, emotions, and the present moment.

I am at peace, familiar with calmness, and I automatically choose to see the best in all people and their positive intentions in life. Research into ayahuasca has shown that it can be particularly effective in treating conditions like PTSD, depression, and addiction. The brew's psychoactive effects are believed to allow individuals to access repressed memories, emotions, and trauma, helping them to process and integrate these experiences into their conscious awareness.

The guidance of an experienced shaman or therapist during these ceremonies is crucial, as it ensures that the healing process is supported, and the individual is safely navigated through their journey

Psilocybin Mushrooms

Psilocybin, the active compound in "magic mushrooms," has been used in various cultures for centuries as a tool for spiritual and emotional healing. Recent studies have highlighted its potential to reduce symptoms of depression, anxiety, and existential distress, especially in individuals facing terminal illness. Psilocybin works by altering the brain's default mode network, which is associated with the sense of self and ego.

This disruption allows for a temporary dissolution of the ego, leading to what many describe as a "mystical experience"—a sense of unity with the universe, deep interconnectedness, and an altered perception of reality.

These experiences can be incredibly healing, as they often allow individuals to view their trauma from a new, detached perspective. The emotional release and insights gained during a psilocybin session can lead to long-lasting changes in behavior and mindset, promoting a sense of peace and acceptance. Although my friends and I used "shrooms" recreationally in our younger days, it wasn't until I was on my healing journey that I began to consume them for ceremony and healing, embarking on what I would call a journey.

The Role of Set and Setting

It's important to emphasize that the healing potential of these substances is highly dependent on the "set and setting"—the mindset of the individual and the environment in which the experience takes place. A supportive, safe, and guided environment is essential for a positive and therapeutic experience. Without these conditions, the intense nature of psychedelic experiences can lead to negative outcomes, such as "bad trips" or re-traumatization.

To prepare for our ayahuasca ceremony, we underwent a two-week or longer cleanse, reducing internet and device use, avoiding sugar and spice, reducing meat consumption, abstaining from sexual activity, avoiding pork, spending time in nature, and so forth to prepare for our journey and enter the ceremony space with the right intentions.

Having sharing circles as part of the ceremony can also be beneficial, allowing participants to share as a group in a circle and have one-on-one time with the shaman.

I will be forever grateful for having access to these alternative medicines and witnessing their positive effects on the lives of my friends who also participated in the ceremonies. My friends and I who have participated in such ceremonies are doing well, and it is pleasing to see. This doesn't mean that we always have it together, but we are handling life well.

Handling life well doesn't mean that everything is perfect; it means we've learned to navigate challenges with resilience, mindfulness, and a deeper sense of connection to ourselves and others. This journey has taught me to release control over the external things that I cannot change and to surrender to the process, trusting that things will always work out as they should. Embracing this mindset has brought a profound sense of peace and allowed me to focus on what truly matters—internal growth and well-being.

Our journey of self-acceptance has also empowered us to step out of our comfort zones and pursue great things, even when they scare us. We may not always feel ready, but we move forward anyway, knowing that growth often lies on the other side of fear. It's this willingness to face the unknown, coupled with a deep trust in ourselves and the process, that has enabled us to continue thriving, no matter what challenges come our way.

Integration and Long-Term Healing

One of the critical aspects of using psychedelics and plant medicines for healing is the integration process that follows the experience. Integration involves taking the insights and emotions that arise during the psychedelic journey and applying them to everyday life. This process often requires ongoing therapy, journaling, meditation, and other practices that support emotional processing and personal growth. It's also important to continue to be mindful of your "set and setting" even after the psychedelic experience. The mental, emotional, and physical environments you cultivate post-experience can significantly influence how well you integrate your insights. Surrounding yourself with supportive people and maintaining a healthy lifestyle are key components of successful integration.

Disclaimer: The information provided in this chapter is based on personal experiences and research. It is important to note that the use of psychedelics and plant medicines should be approached with caution and respect. This content is not intended to replace professional medical advice, diagnosis, or treatment. Always consult with a qualified healthcare professional before considering any form of psychedelic therapy or plant medicine.

The guidance of a trained professional is crucial to ensure safety and maximize the therapeutic benefits of these practices. References for where the facts and information in this chapter comes from is listed at the back of this book for your convenience.

Before Birth: My Journey Through Trauma
Even before my first breath, trauma touched my life. The emotional turmoil experienced in the womb left lasting impacts on my growth and resilience.

In the lead-up to one of the healing retreats that I attended, I decided to explore my sugar addiction. The shaman suggested that I investigate the time when I was in my mother's womb and the state of my parents' marriage at that time.

At birth, I was adopted by my biological mother's brother (my biological uncle), as he couldn't have children of his own and had asked his sister (my mother) if he could whangai me.

Whangai is the Māori term for adoption within the extended family. From a young age, I was aware of this arrangement, but what I discovered for the first time in my 40s was that my biological mother had been unfaithful in her marriage. This revelation explained why my biological father was more than willing to give me away (adopt me out).

When I learned of this, I became instantly emotional, crying at the thought that I wasn't wanted even before I was born. Additionally, not receiving my mother's breast milk at birth led to my seeking comfort in the form of sugar.

The Path Ahead

The trauma of hearing my parents argue and experiencing my mother's disloyalty while in the womb contributed to a lifelong fear of rejection and not being wanted. This need for belonging impacted my ability to maintain intimate relationships and close friendships in my early life, as I feared abandonment.

It's amazing to realize that trauma experienced in the womb can have such a profound impact on one's life. These early experiences of feeling unwanted and fearing rejection significantly affected my adult life, leading to low self-esteem and a persistent fear of vulnerability. This, in turn, hindered the development of healthy relationships and career success, creating deep-seated insecurities and making me more susceptible to marijuana addiction and being a people pleaser. The reluctance to pursue opportunities due to the fear of further rejection or failure was a direct consequence of this early trauma.

My trauma continued after birth as my first stepmother, Addie Perston (who loved me dearly) and my grandmother (who was influential in my first infant years) passed away before I turned five.

By the age of seven, I had a second stepmother who was physically and verbally abusive towards me, treating me unfairly and like a servant in the house.

She never allowed me to express my emotions and would punish me harshly if I cried from the hurt caused by her words. I wouldn't wish that sort of abuse I had at that age on any child. I was only 9 or 10 years old at the time.

Because I suppressed my emotions as a child, I struggled with anger management as an adult. Despite all the work I've done on myself, and as much as I don't want to be this way, I still occasionally deal with passive-aggressive tendencies. (Feb, 2025).

Emotional Intelligence in Trauma and Healing

As we delve deeper into the journey of overcoming trauma, it's essential to explore the role of emotional intelligence. The concept of emotional intelligence (EI) was popularized by Daniel Goleman, an American psychologist, in his 1995 book *Emotional Intelligence: Why It Can Matter More Than IQ*. However, the term "emotional intelligence" was first introduced by researchers Peter Salovey and John D. Mayer in their 1990 article titled 'Emotional Intelligence.'

Emotional intelligence, often defined as the ability to recognize, manage and understand our own emotions and those of others, is a powerful tool in the healing process. When we experience trauma, our emotional landscape can become turbulent and challenging to navigate. By developing emotional intelligence, we gain the skills to identify and process these complex emotions, fostering a sense of control and resilience.

This not only aids in our personal healing but also enhances our relationships and overall wellbeing. In the following section, we will discuss how to cultivate emotional intelligence.

1.   **Name It to Tame It:**

Recognizing and naming your emotions can help you manage and understand them better. This approach involves identifying what you are feeling which can reduce the intensity of your emotions and provide clarity. For example, if you feel anxious, say to yourself, "I am feeling anxious". You can fully experience the feeling when you are able to language it.

2.   **Its Yours To own**

Instead of blaming others for the feeling you chose to have, connect with the truth of that feeling which comes from within. Your feeling is your own responsibility, no one else's. No one makes you feel the way you feel. Owning your feeling is the precursor to acceptance, change, and empowerment.

3.   **Feel to Heal:**

Allow yourself to fully experience your emotions without suppression, guilt or shame. The only reason we want to avoid a feeling is due to the first times when we experienced those emotions or feelings. We start to think we are the only ones experiencing this and that it is not normal to have such emotions. Know that guilt or shame comes from our conditioning. When we accept the feeling, we reclaim our energy.

If there is discomfort, allow it. If you need to cry then do so. Journaling or talking with a trusted friend or therapist can help process these feelings.

4.   **Let it be and Let it Go:**

Embracing your emotions can lead to emotional release and healing. Once we remove the resistance of the feeling we allow it to be. Feelings are designed to be short-lived. It may last a minute or two, it may last for hours. There is no rule here except to accept and allow. Connect with the feeling as if it's part of you and be there with the feeling like you would be there for a child.

What is it that you need to do to let it go? Is it to stamp your feet, shake your body, scream, cry, shout, yell, punch a punching bag, kick a ball, run, star jumps etc... Whatever you do to release the feeling, make sure it is healthy and safe.

Take Your Mask off

The reason I have included the following model in this chapter is that it resonates deeply with the journey of healing. As we heal, we begin to reconnect with our true, authentic self at our core. The Core, Crud, Crust model shown here is by Remi Pearson. She emphasizes this process, highlighting the importance of confronting and addressing the guilt and shame we often mask.

The Path Ahead

It's important to mention that my next statement isn't from Remi but my own observation when I say this, like healing, the Core, Crud, Crust model illustrates that we must endure pain to find pleasure and navigate through darkness to truly appreciate the light. This model helps individuals reconnect with their true selves by understanding and addressing the layers that obscure their core identity. Pearson developed this model to guide people through peeling back the layers of "crud" and "crust" accumulated from negative self-talk, limiting beliefs, and societal conditioning, ultimately revealing the core—the authentic self. Our ultimate goal is to be our authentic self at our core.

The CRUD is where the hurt is. People spend so much energy here. If you don't acknowledge your hurt you'll never get to the core of who you are

At the CORE is who we truly are at our authentic self. This is where our core values & wildest dreams sit.

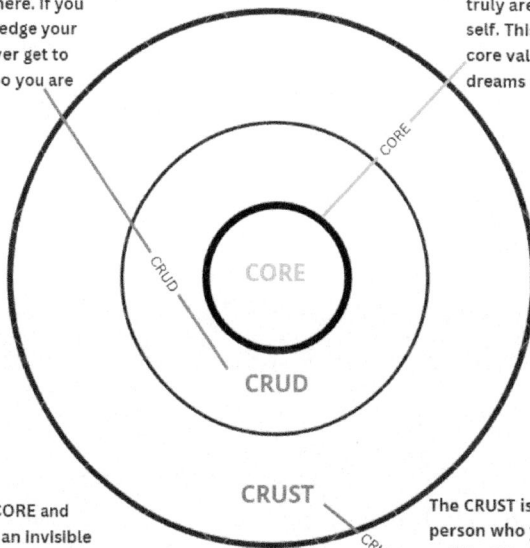

CORE

CRUD

CRUST

CORE

CRUD

CRUST

Between the CORE and CRUD there is an invisible protection shield that is there to protect your Core

The CRUST is the fake person who you put out in public. This is the mask, like a disguise 'so we don't' get to be our true self

Trauma

Core: The Core represents our true essence, where we are deeply connected to ourselves, others, and the world around us in a meaningful way. This core identity is pure, whole, and complete, akin to the state we are in when we are born. At this stage, we possess an innate sense of confidence and curiosity. We don't know how to judge ourselves or procrastinate; we simply explore the world with an open heart and a fearless spirit.

At our core, we embody qualities of care, strength, and connection, with love being at the very center. These attributes define our true identity, representing the real "you" before any external influences or experiences shape us. As infants, we approach life with a sense of adventure and a 'can-do' attitude. We are willing to try new things without fear of failure or rejection. Consider how we as a baby learnt to crawl, walk, and eventually run. Despite numerous falls and failures, the child continues to try until they succeed, driven by innate curiosity and determination.

At our core, we also have a natural propensity for laughter and a comfort in seeking support from others. This stage of life is marked by an absence of fear, an eagerness to explore, and a pure, undiluted form of self-expression. As we grow older, layers of "crud" and "crust" begin to form around our core due to various life experiences, trauma, negative self-talk, and societal conditioning.

These layers can obscure our true selves, making it challenging to reconnect with our core identity. from our Core, a place of love, strength, and connection, we are initially untainted by external influences. However, as we grow, the adults in our lives introduce us to commands like "no" and "stop," and we begin to encounter the three universal fears: rejection, judgment, and failure.

These experiences can bring about feelings of shame, causing us to lose touch with our core qualities. As a result, we start to identify with the Crud, which consists of negative beliefs and self-talk accumulated over time.

These internalized voices tell us we are not good enough, capable, or worthy. This layer often forms in response to criticism and negative experiences, creating emotional and psychological baggage that distorts our self-perception and conditions our thinking, leading to the creation of a false identity.

Crud: The CRUD is

> The stuff you do not want others to know about.
>
> The shameful stuff that you make up in your mind and strongly start to believe in.
>
> The shame you may have around your family.
>
> The story you tell yourself that you aren't good enough because…

Trauma

The issue with the "Crud" is that we expend so much energy trying to cover it up that we end up being someone we're not, instead of embracing who we truly are. We will never reach our "Core" if we don't address the "Crud." By confronting our fear and shame, we uncover our inner strength and true light, becoming awakened.

The goal is to reach your core (the pleasure), and to do so, we must navigate through the crud (the pain) – "on the other side of pain is always pleasure."

As babies, we look up to the adults in our lives with forgiveness and love, eager to show our value and worth. However, when we hear commands like

"Stop that!,"

"Don't do that!,"

"You can't," or "You're too small,"

they affect us emotionally and impact our core. These negative messages contribute to the formation of the crud, which masks our true selves and hinders our growth. We become ashamed of what we did and start to develop a sense of "I am not good enough," "I do not belong," and "I am not loved," which stem from the universal fears of being rejected, judged, and failing.

Brené Brown, a renowned specialist, author, and public speaker on shame and vulnerability, emphasizes that understanding the impact of shame and practicing empathy deepens our humanity and connectedness. Her research highlights that vulnerability is a strength and embracing it can lead to greater emotional resilience and authentic connections. Brown also underscores the power of empathy in healing shame and fostering deeper interpersonal relationships.

"Staying vulnerable is a <u>risk</u> we have to take if we want to experience connection." —Brené Brown

Crust:

Charles Cooley, an American sociologist, introduced the concept of the "looking-glass self," which suggests that we see ourselves as we think others see us. As children, when we are told "no" repeatedly, we internalize it as "I'm wrong," leading to feelings of shame and inadequacy.

This forms the layer of "Crud," where we start believing negative self-talk like, "I am a loser," "I am useless," or "I am a problem." This concept aligns with the idea of the "Crust," a mask we develop to protect the parts of us that have been in pain for a long time. To avoid exposing our perceived inadequacies, we adopt this false disguise. This mask is what we present to the public, hiding what is truly going on beneath the surface. Removing this mask requires vulnerability, courage, and daring.

Trauma

Beneath the surface, there might be family secrets you don't want anyone to know or personal struggles you hide from friends for fear of judgment. Public ridicule can damage self-esteem, leading to a fear of failure and the belief that you are not good enough. To protect ourselves, we wear a mask or play roles we think will be more acceptable, rather than being our true selves.

This continuous cycle reinforces the mask we wear, distancing us further from our true selves. This is why I strive to avoid judging others and to show compassion to everyone I meet, as I firmly believe people are often hurting and need to be heard and seen. With an understanding of the Core, Crud, Crust model we've just explored, you're empowered to realize that people's anger often stems from their own internal struggles and past experiences, not from anything you've done.

When I encounter individuals exhibiting harmful behavior, I can't help but wonder what they might have gone through. Similarly, when I visit a store and see a teller who seems uninterested or miserable, I find myself thinking about what might be on their mind at that moment.

Self-Reflection Questions

- Do you recognize any unhealed trauma affecting your current behavior or emotions?

- What steps can you take today to start addressing and healing from past traumas?

- Who are trusted individuals or professionals you can reach out to for support?

Reframe the Emotional Meaning:

Identify the events that have caused you pain and consciously reframe the emotional meanings you've attached to them. This involves viewing the event from a different perspective and finding a more empowering interpretation. For example, you might see a painful experience as an opportunity for growth and resilience rather than a permanent setback.

Mindfulness and Meditation:

Stay in the present moment. Practice mindfulness and meditation to stay present and connected with your emotions. These practices can help you observe your thoughts and feelings without judgment, reducing stress and enhancing emotional regulation.

Seek Professional Help:

If trauma feels overwhelming, seek the help of a therapist, counsellor, or life coach who can provide guidance and support. Professional help can offer tailored strategies and interventions to help you work through your trauma effectively.

Reflection: Think about the adjective that you would use to describe a baby or a child. They have love, playfulness, creativity, laughter, and they love to tap into exploring new things. They give new things a go without the fear of failure or getting it wrong, they do not worry about what others may think of them. A child gets back up and tries again.

List 5 Now:

1 ....

2 ....

3 ....

4 ....

5 ....

Which of these childhood attributes are you using or need to use in your life today?

_____

Conclusion

The journey from darkness to light through trauma and healing is challenging yet profoundly transformative. By understanding the roots of trauma, recognizing its manifestations, and engaging in active healing, we can reclaim our lives, rediscover our core selves, and foster resilience. Healing is not just about overcoming past pain; it's about rebuilding our authentic self and, in doing so, opening the door to deeper connections—with ourselves and others.

As we peel back the layers of CRUD and CRUST that obscure our true essence, we embark on a journey toward wholeness and empowerment. The Core, Crud, Crust model teaches us that our deepest self, our core, may be hidden by the weight of past experiences, yet by facing these painful layers, we can reclaim the peace and authenticity that lie beneath.

This process demands vulnerability and the courage to face fears, but in doing so, we pave the way for personal growth, freedom, and fulfillment. Yet healing doesn't happen in isolation. As we move toward healing ourselves, our relationships become a reflection of that growth. Our connections with others—whether intimate, familial, or platonic—play an integral role in the healing process.

Trauma

The healthier our relationship with ourselves, the more we can contribute positively to those around us. In the next chapter, we'll explore how relationships serve as both mirrors and catalysts for our healing. Whether through the love we offer or the challenges we face within them, relationships are fundamental to our personal journey

As you heal your inner wounds and reconnect with your true self, you'll find that your capacity to build meaningful, fulfilling relationships deepens. Prepare to examine how the bonds we form, the way we love, and the connection we build with others—especially with ourselves—create the foundation for a fulfilling, resilient life. Let's journey into how healthy relationships, grounded in self-love and understanding, can be the path to deeper healing and personal growth. Embracing your emotions can lead to emotional release and healing.

CHAPTER SEVEN

Relationships

The Path to Healing

Your actions reflect your priorities. What are you willing to fight for today?-
Garett J White

Healthy relationships are the cornerstone of a fulfilling life, providing emotional support and stability. Healthy relationships help you navigate challenges, celebrate successes, and foster a sense of belonging. Although building and maintaining quality relationships requires effort and sometimes involves pain, the rewards are immeasurable. Whether you're a parent, single, married, or simply seeking to improve your personal relationships, the insights shared here will benefit you, as these principles are universal.

Relationships

The Power of Self-Love in Relationships

Self-love ultimately leads to healthier and more balanced relationships. It empowers you to contribute positively to your connections, fostering mutual respect and deeper bonds. When you truly love yourself, you no longer depend on others for validation or emotional support. This self-assurance allows you to approach relationships from a place of strength and stability, rather than neediness or insecurity. In building strong, healthy intimate relationships, self-love, which is a form of self-acceptance, is crucial. As you cultivate self-love, you become more capable of meeting the emotional needs of others. A man with this level of self-confidence is better equipped to understand and respond to the emotional needs of others, especially his partner, which is highly attractive to women.

If someone lacks love, respect, or acceptance for themselves, they become reliant on others to feel good, which hinders their ability to be fully present with others' emotional needs. They lack the confidence to take risks, playing it safe in life and missing out on its greatest opportunities.

Now that you've explored the tools and resources in this book that have helped you find contentment with who you are, you are ready to engage in relationships with genuine interest and affection, rather than using others to fill 'your' emotional gaps.

When was the last time you treated yourself or took yourself out for dinner?

What activities can you engage in that don't require your partner to be present?

Do you need to pick up a hobby you've abandoned, or is there something new you'd like to learn?

Giving back to yourself regularly, even if it's just a 5-minute walk around the block each evening, is essential for maintaining a strong sense of self.

Father-Son Relationship

The father-son relationship plays a pivotal role in the emotional and psychological development of boys and men. Research indicates that a positive father figure is crucial for healthy emotional growth, while the absence of a father or a negative father-son relationship can contribute to issues such as anger, depression, and difficulty forming healthy relationships in adulthood.

Studies have shown that boys who grow up with an unhealthy relationship with their father are at higher risk for various negative outcomes, including behavioral problems, lower self-esteem, and challenges in maintaining healthy intimate relationships. The nature of an unhealthy father-son relationship can vary. A father might have been frequently absent due to work, struggled with addiction or mental health issues, or perhaps passed away when the boy was very young.

On the more severe end of the spectrum, the father could have been a narcissist or abusive—verbally, mentally, or physically. In some cases, the father may have lacked the self-love necessary to meet his son's emotional needs. As I mentioned earlier in this book, I was adopted at birth, and what I didn't share was how tumultuous my relationship with my stepfather (whom I call "Dad" today) was. Although dad was physically present during my childhood, his alcoholism prevented him from being emotionally available to me. His alcoholism led to domestic violence in the home, which ingrained a deep-seated trauma response in me whenever I heard couples arguing. Sadly, my father never attended my sports days or school events, and even in my adult life, when he was no longer an alcoholic, he remained absent from significant moments in my life. As a result, I grew up without a positive father figure, which instilled in me a lack of self-worth and a belief that I wasn't loved.

It wasn't until my late 30s that I realized this had subconsciously created a fear of entering a long-term intimate relationship or starting my own family. The idea of being a father scared me because I doubted whether I could be good enough to be a father, let alone a husband.

The Power of Forgiveness

At the start of my personal journey, when I participated in various healing modalities, one of the first exercises I implemented was forgiveness, which led me to forgiving my parents.

Using strategies like positive "I AM" affirmation exercises and overcoming limiting beliefs—taught in Chapter Three: *Identity*—I rewrote the narrative I had created about my relationship with my dad. I reframed our defining moments, recognizing that he did his best with what he had, understanding that his lack of parenting skills (based on my personal terms) was a result of generational trauma.

This realization brought me great relief and a newfound sense of courage and self-belief began to grow within me. I once believed my experience was unique and that I was the only one who went through what I did as a child, but it's a common story, more widespread than one might realize.

Let's consider Robert Downey Jr.'s story as an example.

Case Story: Robert Downey Jr.'s Journey Through Family and Addiction

Robert Downey Jr.'s relationship with his father, Robert Downey Sr., was marked by substance abuse and instability. Introduced to drugs at a young age by his father, Downey Jr. struggled with addiction for many years. However, through personal development and a commitment to breaking the cycle of trauma, he transformed his life and career. His journey underscores the power of self-awareness and resilience in overcoming a troubled past, demonstrating that healing and growth are possible despite early challenges.

By recognizing the patterns from his upbringing and committing to personal growth, Robert Downey Jr. was able to rebuild his life and career. Whether you relate to my story or Downey Jr.'s, these stories demonstrate that it is possible to overcome a troubled past through forgiveness and self-improvement, leading to meaningful change and healthier relationships.

Breaking the Cycle: How Perspective Shapes Destiny

Reflect on your own life—what patterns or behaviors have you inherited that no longer serve you? Once you identify these patterns, you can make conscious choices to change them. What would happen if you did the changes? What wouldn't happen if you did the changes?

The key to breaking the cycle is awareness. Jim Rohn, a renowned motivational speaker, often shared a powerful story about two brothers who grew up with an alcoholic father. One brother became an alcoholic, saying, "Because my father was an alcoholic." The other chose a different path, abstaining from alcohol entirely, and his reason was the same: "Because my father was an alcoholic." This story illustrates the power of choice and perspective in shaping our lives. While our past may influence us, it doesn't have to define our future. No matter the challenges of your upbringing, you have the power to choose a different path. It's about recognizing that your past experiences are part of your story, but they don't have to dictate your future.

You can use your past as a catalyst for positive change, making decisions that align with the life you want to create. As a child, you are not responsible for what happened to you, but as an adult, you are 100% responsible for what you do with your life.

In my own family, despite similar upbringings, the choices between my siblings and I led us down very different paths. Some of us pursued education and personal growth, while others struggled with substance abuse and depression. This contrast reinforces the idea that while our environment shapes us, it doesn't have to determine our destiny. The choices you make today can break the cycle for future generations. By choosing growth, integrity, and self-awareness, you not only transform your life but also set a powerful example for your children and those around you. The path to a better future starts with the decisions you make right now.

Inherited Patterns: Your Childhood on Adult Relationships
The patterns and behaviors you experienced growing up can deeply influence your current actions and reactions. Recognizing this connection is empowering. By understanding the impact of your upbringing, you can begin to break the cycle of negativity and create a healthier environment for yourself and your family.

In my line of work, I often meet men who present me with the problems they are experiencing in their marriage and family life. Almost every time, when I ask about the relationship they had with their own father, they reveal that it wasn't a good one.

Relationships

This re-occuring pattern underscores the profound influence that a father's presence—or absence—can have on a man's ability to parent effectively. A man who struggles to be an effective husband or father often carries unresolved issues and negative experiences from his past.

Trauma can have a profound impact on the lives of men who struggle with relationships and quality parenting. The traumatic experiences of your past can manifest as toxic habits, emotional suppression, and difficulties in connecting with your children and partners.

Let's examine how the childhood relationship with a father affected another well-known figure.

Case Story: Donald Trump— Childhood Trauma and Adult Behavior

Donald Trump's childhood was shaped by his father, Fred Trump, who was authoritarian and emotionally distant. This harsh environment contributed to deep-seated fears of rejection and a need for validation in Donald's adult life, often manifesting as narcissistic behavior. Trump's story highlights how unresolved childhood trauma can impact adult relationships and behavior. It serves as a reminder of the importance of addressing emotional wounds early to prevent them from shaping one's future in negative ways.

Understanding Donald Trump's childhood trauma underscores the importance of addressing early emotional wounds to prevent harmful behaviors later in life. His story illustrates how childhood experiences shape adult behavior and emphasizes the critical need for emotional support and healthy relationships during our formative years, especially from ages 0 to 8. As Dr. Gabor Maté notes, childhood trauma often leads to a perception of the world as dangerous and untrustworthy, attributes that Donald Trump displays.

By recognizing these patterns and taking proactive steps to address them, you can break the cycle and create a healthier, more supportive environment for yourself and your family. Remember, the quality of your relationship reflects the effort and care you invest in it every day.

Reflection Time – Take time here to reflect and to take down notes on anything that may have resonated with you so far in this chapter. Identify an area of your relationship that needs more attention?

Notes....

The Warrior Code

Garrett J. White, founder of Wake-Up Warrior, emphasizes the importance of integrity and commitment in building healthy relationships. He states, "The Warrior has a code. He operates from a place of honor and integrity, not just for himself, but for his family. By committing to this code, he creates an environment where love and connection can thrive

White, an entrepreneur, motivational speaker, and author, is known for his passionate approach to personal development, focusing on helping men become the best versions of themselves. His insights on maintaining relationships are invaluable for anyone looking to strengthen their bonds with their partners. Here are some of his key tips:

1. **Operate from a Place of Integrity:** Always be truthful and transparent with your partner. Honesty builds trust and lays the foundation for a strong relationship.

2. **Commit to the Relationship:** Show unwavering commitment to your partner. This means being present, engaged, and supportive, even during challenging times.

3. **Communicate Effectively:** Open and honest communication is crucial. Share your thoughts, feelings, and concerns openly, and listen actively to your partner.

4. **Show Appreciation and Gratitude:** Regularly express your appreciation for your partner. Acknowledging their efforts and expressing gratitude strengthens the bond between you.

5. **Be Supportive:** Be your partner's biggest supporter. Encourage their personal growth and be there for them in both good times and bad.

6. **Prioritize Quality Time:** Spend quality time together, free from distractions. This helps maintain a strong connection and deepens your relationship.

7. **Resolve Conflicts Respectfully:** Disagreements are natural, but it's important to address them respectfully and constructively. Focus on finding solutions rather than winning arguments.

8. **Maintain Physical and Emotional Intimacy:** Physical closeness and emotional intimacy are vital for a healthy relationship. Make an effort to maintain both aspects.

Incorporating these principles into your relationship creates a strong foundation of trust, respect, and love. By committing to integrity, effective communication, and mutual support, you not only strengthen your bond but also foster an environment where both you and your partner can thrive.

How to Avoid the Pitfalls of Relationship Breakdowns

John Gottman, a renowned psychologist and researcher, has provided key insights into what makes intimate relationships healthy and lasting. His research is invaluable for anyone looking to strengthen their relationship with their partner. Here's a breakdown of his most important findings:

The Four Horsemen: Gottman identified four communication patterns—criticism, contempt, defensiveness, and stonewalling—that are so harmful they can predict relationship breakdowns with over 90% accuracy. If these patterns appear in your relationship, addressing them early is crucial to prevent further damage:

- **Criticism:** Attacking your partner's character instead of addressing specific behaviors.
- **Contempt:** Displaying disrespect or a sense of superiority, which is the most damaging of the four.
- **Defensiveness:** Reacting to conflict by counterattacking or playing the victim.
- **Stonewalling:** Shutting down or withdrawing during a conflict, leaving issues unresolved.

- **Key Insight:** Self-love and self-awareness can help you avoid these destructive patterns and communicate more effectively with your partner.

The Magic Ratio: 5:1 Positive to Negative Interactions: Gottman says that the key to long-term success lies in the balance between positive and negative interactions. Couples who maintain a ratio of at least 5 positive interactions for every 1 negative interaction, particularly during conflicts, are far more likely to stay together. This "magic ratio" underscores the importance of nurturing positivity in everyday exchanges, to create a buffer that protect relationships from inevitable challenges and disagreements.

- **Key Insight:** Cultivating self-love and emotional resilience makes it easier to contribute positively to your relationship, helping maintain this crucial balance.

Bids for Connection: In his groundbreaking research, Gottman introduced the concept of "bids"—small, everyday gestures or comments through which one partner seeks attention, affirmation, or emotional connection from the other. These bids can be as simple as a smile, a question, or a touch, but how a partner responds to them is incredibly telling. Whether you turn toward, away, or against these bids plays a crucial role in determining the success of your relationship, as consistent positive responses build trust and intimacy, while negative or indifferent reactions can lead to disconnection and dissatisfaction.

- **Key Insight:** When you're secure in your self-worth, you're more likely to recognize and respond positively to your partner's bids, which strengthens your connection.

Relationships

Emotional Bank Account: Think of your relationship as having an "emotional bank account." Positive interactions deposit goodwill, while negative ones withdraw from it. A high balance, built through kindness, understanding, and affection, helps your relationship weather tough times.

- **Key Insight:** Investing in self-love and personal growth gives you the emotional resources to consistently make positive deposits into your relationship.

The Power of Repair Attempts: Gottman's research highlights the vital role of "repair attempts" in maintaining a healthy relationship. These are efforts made by one partner to deescalate tension during a conflict, whether through humor, a kind word, or a gesture of reconciliation. Successful repair attempts are one of the strongest predictors of long-term relationship success, as they help prevent conflicts from causing lasting damage and foster a sense of security and understanding between partners.

- **Key Insight:** Self-love enhances your ability to initiate and accept repair attempts, helping you navigate conflicts without causing lasting damage.

Shared Meaning and Rituals: Gottman emphasizes the importance of creating shared meaning through rituals, traditions, and shared goals. These shared experiences not only strengthen your bond but also give your relationship a sense of purpose and direction. Whether it's a weekly date night, celebrating special milestones, or working together toward common objectives, these rituals create a deeper connection and foster a shared identity as a couple.

- **Key Insight:** A strong sense of self and clear personal values make it easier for you to contribute to and participate in creating shared meaning with your partner.

Nurturing your relationships can bring profound joy and fulfillment into your life. It's never too late to strengthen the connections that matter most. Start today by taking small, intentional steps to show love, practice empathy, and communicate openly with those around you. Whether it's reaching out to someone you've lost touch with, practicing self-love, or breaking a cycle that no longer serves you, every action counts.

The power to transform your relationships and your life is within you. Embrace it and take the first step toward creating the life and connections you truly desire.

The Importance of Stress Management

Managing stress effectively is crucial for maintaining healthy relationships and being the best version of yourself as a husband and father. Chronic stress can negatively impact your physical and mental health, leading to irritability, fatigue, and difficulty concentrating—all of which can strain your relationships. When stress is unmanaged, it often spills over into interactions with loved ones, creating tension and conflict. On the other hand, by practicing stress management techniques, you can maintain a calm and balanced demeanor, which is essential for effective communication and emotional connection.

Here are some practical strategies for managing stress:

- **Mindfulness and Meditation:** Practicing mindfulness or meditation can help you stay present and reduce stress. These practices allow you to respond thoughtfully rather than react impulsively during stressful situations.

- **Physical Activity:** Regular exercise is a powerful stress reliever. It helps to release endorphins, which improve mood and reduce feelings of anxiety.

- **Time Management:** Organizing your time effectively can prevent the overwhelm that leads to stress. Prioritizing tasks and setting realistic goals can help you manage your responsibilities without feeling stretched too thin.

- **Social Support:** Connecting with friends, family, or a support group can provide emotional relief and a different perspective on the challenges you face.

- **Relaxation Techniques:** Techniques such as deep breathing, progressive muscle relaxation, or yoga can help reduce physical tension and promote relaxation.

According to the American Psychological Association, managing stress is not just about reducing the negative effects but also about building resilience. Developing healthy coping strategies allows you to handle life's challenges more effectively, which in turn, strengthens your relationships. By incorporating stress management techniques into your daily routine, you'll be better equipped to handle the demands of life, ensuring that you can remain balanced, resilient, and fully present in all aspects of your life. For more information, you can refer to the APA's resources on stress management www.apa.org/topic/stress.

Feminine and Masculine Energy

Understanding the balance between feminine and masculine energies is crucial for fostering healthy relationships and achieving personal growth. These energies are not tied to gender but rather represent different aspects of our inner selves that everyone possesses. By learning to recognize and harness these energies, individuals can create more harmonious relationships and lead more fulfilling lives.

In *The Way of the Superior Man: A Spiritual Guide to Mastering the Challenges of Women, Work, and Sexual Desire,* David Deida explores the interplay of feminine and masculine energies within relationships, emphasizing that a healthy dynamic requires a harmonious balance of both. Masculine energy, often associated

Relationships

direction, purpose, and strength, provides stability and structure. Feminine energy, characterized by fluidity, nurturing, and emotional expression, brings warmth and connection.

In a relationship, a person can meet their partner's needs by embracing both energies, creating a secure yet emotionally rich environment. For example, one can use their masculine energy to make decisions with confidence, ensuring that their partner feels safe and protected. Simultaneously, they can tap into their feminine energy by being emotionally present, actively listening, and offering empathy when the partner needs to express their feelings. This balanced approach allows them to be both a strong leader and a compassionate partner.

Deida suggests that understanding when to embody each energy is key to deepening intimacy and fostering mutual respect. By doing so, one can cultivate a relationship that is both dynamic and fulfilling for both partners. Ultimately, this dance between masculine and feminine energies creates a powerful synergy that enhances the overall connection and harmony in the relationship.

For more insights on understanding feminine and masculine energies or to learn more about *The Way of the Superior Man: A Spiritual Guide to Mastering the Challenges of Women, Work, and Sexual Desire* you can explore the book directly or visit David Deida's official website https://deida.info/.

Relationships

Conclusion:

Throughout this chapter, we've explored the profound impact relationships have on our emotional and psychological well-being. Whether it's the importance of self-love or the intricate dynamics between fathers and sons, we've seen how past experiences shape our current relationships. Relationships, when nurtured with intention and care, provide the foundation for a fulfilling life. But relationships don't thrive on emotions alone. How we communicate within those relationships has a significant impact on their strength and quality. The language we use—whether verbal or nonverbal—shapes our interactions, builds or breaks trust, and defines the level of intimacy we experience.

Just as we've seen how healing past wounds can lead to deeper connections, effective communication is the key to maintaining those connections.

In the next chapter, we'll dive into the power of language and how mastering the art of communication can transform your relationships. Words have the ability to heal, connect, and inspire, and learning how to use them wisely will take your relationships to the next level. Let's explore how language can be a tool for building stronger bonds and creating lasting, meaningful connections.

CHAPTER EIGHT

Language

Rewriting Your Narrative for Success

"Without knowing the force of words, it is impossible to know men."
- Confucius

How Language Can Shape Your Life

Changing your life starts with changing your words. The language you use can shape your experiences, either limiting or expanding your opportunities. Words have the power to evoke laughter, anger, happiness, and tears—they can wound or heal. Choosing words of encouragement and self-compassion can boost your self-esteem and confidence.

The language we use influences our thoughts, emotions, and actions. Words form and change our beliefs, offering us either hope or destruction. The way we communicate with others also plays a crucial role. Respectful, kind, and empathetic language fosters healthier relationships and more meaningful interactions with your children, spouse, and colleagues, creating a supportive social network. Years into my personal development journey, I realized that I tend to see the best in situations where others see chaos. My problems often seem small compared to those of my inner circle, and I am fearless in moments when others are filled with fear. After reading *Awaken the Giant Within* by Tony Robbins, I understood that the reason I appeared extraordinary to others was due to the way I used words, especially in self-talk and when describing my experiences.

As I grew, my language evolved from "I can't," "that's too difficult," and "maybe next time" to "I can," "I'm open to trying," and "let's do this." I became more precise in expressing my feelings— recognizing when I was merely uncomfortable rather than angry or surprised rather than offended.

Even in moments that seem impossible to explain, I shifted from saying, "I can't believe it," to "Thank you for this delightful surprise; I deserve it." This shift placed me in a state of gratitude and opened me up to receiving more positive experiences. Whether you call these moments blessings or manifestations, the important thing is to avoid limiting your potential by dismissing them as unbelievable.

Throughout history, our greatest leaders, preachers, motivational speakers, and thinkers have harnessed the power of words to transform emotions and ways of thinking.

For instance, when I attended Christopher Howard's event in 2009, his words shifted my emotions from anger to forgiveness, leading me to forgive my parents for my unsettling childhood. This forgiveness immediately increased my sense of self-worth. The truth is, words can shape our destiny, no matter our past or the traumas we've experienced. Words create emotions, which in turn create actions, and from our actions flow the results of our lives. People with a negative vocabulary experience a negative life, limiting their potential, while those with a positive vocabulary enjoy a rich, fulfilling life, painting their experiences with a wide variety of colors.

Words Can Give an Emotional Charge

Think about a time when someone said something that made you angry, furious, or upset. You have the same power over yourself through your self-talk, for better or worse. Language is incredibly powerful, influencing your mindset and the emotional response your body has to your words.

For example, words rooted in love give your body a positive emotional charge, while words like "angry" or "hate" create a very different, negative charge.

To consciously control your life, you need to evaluate and improve your consistent vocabulary, ensuring it propels you in the direction you want rather than where you fear to go.

Language

Using emotionally charged words can magically transform your own state or someone else's. Often, we use words as "shortcuts," but these shortcuts can shortchange us emotionally.

For example, when you feel overwhelmed, it's likely with good reason. Instead of saying, "I'm overwhelmed," try "I'm busy" or "I have a lot to work with right now." This presupposes that you will handle it despite feeling overwhelmed. By reframing the situation this way, you can break the task down into smaller, manageable pieces until it's complete.

When you're confused, try saying, "I'm seeking clarity" or "I still need to understand that." This language shift moves the focus toward finding a solution. Even the word "hope" can be replaced with "trust," as in "I trust your trip went well" instead of "I hope your trip went well." Similarly, replacing "I have to do this" with "I get to do this" transforms a task from an obligation into an opportunity.

Words can either shatter our egos or inflame our hearts. We can instantly change any emotional experience by choosing new words to describe what we're feeling. If we fail to master our language, allowing our word choices to be driven by unconscious habits, our entire life experience can be diminished.

The Path Ahead

The Words You Constantly Select Will Shape Your Destiny

Simply by changing your vocabulary, you can transform how you feel, think, and live. During the global lockdown, when fear and uncertainty were widespread, I chose to describe the experience as an opportunity to reinvent myself.

While others spoke of terror and despair, I spoke of ways to improve my health, losing 16kg with the help of the Isagenix system. This difference in vocabulary led to vastly different experiences, even during the same event. Despite facing criticism for my personal choices to not have the vaccination, I chose to use words like "tickled" and "entertained" rather than "angry" or "frustrated." This word choice kept me in a state that I preferred, helping me maintain a positive outlook.

What other words can you use instead of "angry," "furious," or "livid"? Try "mildly annoyed" or "curious." The emotional charge of these words is different and can change the outcome of a conversation, especially during conflicts with loved ones.

CAPTIVITY OF THE MIND

"Captivity and control come in many forms, but the goal is always the same: to break down the captive's will, to kill any notion of self-worth, and to erase the person's memory of their own soul." - Mariah Carey

135

Language

Language has the profound ability to shape our reality, either empowering us or holding us captive. Limiting language reinforces negative beliefs, confining our potential and stifling our growth.

Phrases like "I can't," "I'm not good enough," or "I'll never succeed" create a mental prison, dictating what we believe is possible. These self-imposed restrictions stem from past experiences, societal expectations, and internalized criticism, creating a narrative we accept as truth

Limiting language perpetuates a cycle of self-doubt and fear, making it difficult to take risks or embrace new opportunities. It diminishes our self-worth and erases our belief in our capabilities. Conversely, by changing our language, we can break free from these mental shackles.

Adopting a growth mindset and using affirmations like "I can learn," "I am capable," and "I will try" can significantly alter our self-perception and open up new possibilities.

Awareness of the language we use daily is crucial. Replacing limiting beliefs with empowering ones is essential for personal growth. When we speak to ourselves with kindness and encouragement, we nurture a positive self-image and foster inner strength.

Redefining our narrative is key to reclaiming control over our lives and achieving our goals.

Words Impact Our Beliefs and Actions

Below is a list of emotions or expressions that are common in our vocabulary. The idea is to use a few transformative words per day or week and gradually expand to more. When you catch yourself about to describe an experience with a negative word, pause.

Be mindful of the feeling associated with that word and consider if there's a better, more empowering word that aligns with your desires. I call this The Vocabulary Game because it can be a lot of fun, playful, and challenging at the same time (just like a game).

Negative Emotion / Expression	Transforms into
I'm feeling…	*I'm feeling…*
Angry	Disenchanted
Pissed off	Tinkled
Embarrassed	Aware
Embarrassed	Stimulated
Exhausted	A little droopy
I hate	I prefer
Impatient	Anticipating
Jealous	Over loving
Lazy	Storing energy
Overloaded	Stretched

Language

Overwhelmed	Busy
Depressed	Calm before action
Depressed	Not on top of it
Confused	Curious
Fear	Wonderment
Fearful	Curious
Insulted	Misunderstood
Hurt	Bothered
Humiliated	Uncomfortable
Furious	Passionate
Failure	Stumble
Failure	Learning
Destroyed	Set back
Painful	Uncomfortable
Sad	Sorting my thoughts
Rejected	Underappreciated
Rejected	Overlooked
Rejected	Misunderstood
Sick	Cleansing
Stupid	Unresourceful
Stupid	Learning
Terrible	Different

The Path Ahead

Now, I wonder if you can add to this list, I'm sure you can, so come up with five words that you habitually use that create negative feelings in your life, and then write a list of alternatives that would either break your pattern by making you laugh because they're so ridiculous, or at least lower the intensity.

Old, un-resourceful word	New, resourceful word

The same technique can be used in reverse. Think of the language you use around pleasure and experiences that give you joy or make you happy. Some people may describe a pleasant experience by saying it is "good" and others may experience the same event and yell "That was *phenomenal*!"

Do you think the people who see the same event as good or phenomenal experience that event in the same way? I needed to expand my vocabulary around positive experiences because I kept using the word "awesome" and I wanted to have access to a plethora of words.

I then came up with *stupendous, mind boggling, out of this world, incredible, outrageous, astonishing* and so forth.

Language

Can you think of any other words you may use as a substitute for the word awesome?

What words could you use as an alternative for the below?

Good	Awesome
Fine	
Excited	
Happy	
Okay	
Like	Love
Pretty Good	
Great	
Satisfied	

Play the vocabulary game with passion and intensity and playfulness for fourteen (14) days and notice the difference it makes. You can use it at your line of work when speaking with colleagues, when you are engaging with your children and complimenting them on their behavior or when it feels like a heated discussion is taking place with a friend or lover. Just for the joy and fun of it, when you are experiencing (rather than confronted with) an interesting (rather than challenging) situation, respond with mild, unbiased and even empowering language.

When experiencing a situation that gives you pleasure, turn up the volume and intensity of your language, make it even more *playful* and *outrageous* and *energized*.

Feel the emotions of the words you choose to use and notice the difference.

Step One: Decide that you will commit to having much more pleasure in your life and a lot less pain. Realise that one of the reasons you have experienced maybe so much pain in the past that has kept you from pleasure is using language that intensifies negative emotion.

Step Two: Get leverage on yourself so that you can use new *transformative* words and develop a new habit of using empowering language. One way to do this is to think of how ridiculous it is to work yourself into a fit of frenzy when you have the choice of feeling good! You could approach three friends and share with them the words that you want to change.

For example, if you get frustrated a lot tell them you have decided to use words like "fascinated" instead of angry or frustrated. Have your friends pull you up when you do use the disempowering words/language and ask them to do it in a supportive way more than criticism.

Even now, when I catch myself using old *disempowering* words I correct myself using words to how I want to feel. After some time, the new language patterns became my consistent approach. My friends would often comment *"wow you really do see positive in all situations"* or they would giggle if they heard me correct myself.

Language

Does this mean you can't be angry? Of course not! Anger can be a very useful emotion. Some men do it really well and some women could learn to do it better. We just don't want our most negative emotions to be our tools of first resort and on a side note it is ok to feel angry and it is not ok to be angry towards anyone. We want to add to our level of choice.

We want to have a greater number and quality of emotions in our lives. Earlier on in this chapter we could look at some useful, empowering alternatives to the word angry.

Step Three: Remember that transformative language isn't just to lower the intensity of negative emotions it can be used to increase the intensity of positive emotions. When someone asks you how you are feeling instead of saying "good", "okay" or "so-so" try saying *"I feel enthralled, "or "I feel spectacular, "or "I feel wonderful".*

As simple as this may sound what it is happening from a scientific point of view it creates a new pattern in your neurology – a new neural highway to pleasure and of course puts you physiologically into a more empowered state of being. Choose three words that you can use as a substitute when answering to the question – how are you? What else could you say instead of "I'm fine," "Things are all right," "I'm feeling good." I have provided some examples to help you spice up your current experience of life.

Circle the ones that you think would be different or fun to add to your vocabulary.

Good Word	Great Word
Alert	Energised
Excited	Ecstatic, impassioned, outrageous
Feeling good	Just tremendous
Fortunate	Unbelievably blessed
Good	Better than excellent
Good	Just doesn't get any better, magic, vibrant
Nice	Spectacular, Fantastic
Pretty Good	Soaring
Resourceful	Brilliant
Happy	Totally blissed, stoked, hyped
Great	Exhilarated, Incredible, exuberant
All right	Superb
Awake	Rearing to go
Curious	Fascinated
Fantastic	Fabulous
Fun	Vivacious
Glad	Over the moon
Terrific	Ecstatic

Language

Conclusion: In professional settings, parenting, or everyday interactions, language plays a critical role in shaping the world around us. By consciously choosing our words, we can turn ordinary statements into powerful affirmations that uplift and inspire. For instance, as a parent, instead of saying, "I'm happy you did that," you might say, "I'm thrilled you cleaned your room." These small shifts in language can transform good words into great ones, as demonstrated earlier. Be mindful of how you use language in all areas of your life. Instead of saying, "I'm starving to death," try, "I feel a little hungry"—unless, of course, you genuinely haven't eaten for a long time. In situations involving health or injury, when someone says, "That looks bad," or "That must be painful," consider responding with, "I am healing and getting stronger by the minute," or "My body is a miracle and is healing itself."

Reframing challenges as opportunities and obstacles as stepping stones empowers you to face life's trials with resilience and optimism. By emphasizing possibilities and potential, you open yourself to new horizons, achieving what once seemed impossible. Now is your moment. Take control of your language. Notice the words you habitually use and replace them with those that empower you. Adjust the emotional intensity as needed. Start today—write down your words, commit to more empowering language, and follow through. Discover how this simple tool can enhance your life experiences in profound ways.

The Path Ahead

Language is more than a means of communication; it shapes your reality and influences how you perceive and interact with the world. This chapter has shown how labels can either limit or expand your experiences, highlighting the importance of choosing words that empower rather than restrict. Through intentional language choices, you can reshape your mindset, face challenges with resilience, and unlock new possibilities. Let this chapter serve as your guide to harnessing the power of words, paving the way for greater personal and interpersonal growth.

As you refine your language to empower yourself and those around you, consider how the words you choose can shape your dreams and the goals you set. In the next chapter, we'll explore how to harness the power of language to envision and achieve your biggest aspirations, turning your dreams into reality.

CHAPTER NINE

Goals

Charting Your Course

"All our dreams can come true, if we have the courage to pursue them"
- *Walt Disney:*

Dream Big

"Imagine and create the greatest dream," Christopher Howard told the auditorium at his coaching event in 2009. "Imagine the biggest, most audacious dream that you have always wanted in your mind and go for it—even if it seems out of reach or impossible right now. Just imagine it, dream it, and feel it," Chris would say.

Since then, I've encountered this message repeatedly, from the teachings of Dr. Joe Dispenza to various personal development events. This is a powerful example of practicing faith—not waiting to see if it will happen, but knowing it will. According to Jim Rohn, an influential American entrepreneur and motivational speaker known for his philosophy on personal development and success, connecting our dreams to our future is often overlooked when people set their goals. Rohn emphasizes that your dreams should be the greatest influence on your daily decisions and activities. When you are clear on your dreams and goals, it will help with the decisions you make today, aligning with the saying from American actor and author Sean Patrick Flanery: "Do something today that your future self will thank you for."

The Power of the Intentional Goals

When your "why" is strong enough, the "how" becomes automatic. When your future excites you, it captures your imagination and significantly influences you. To design a future you dream of living, you must have well-defined and planned goals. Back in 2009, when I created a vision of my big dream future for the first time, I could never have imagined that many of these dreams would come true. From living in a rundown hostel to working on a luxury cruise ship, from dropping out of school to becoming an author, from living in constant anger to finding peace, from binge drinking to living sober—this was just the beginning of the dream I envisioned fifteen years ago. I remember envisioning a future where it wasn't just about what I was doing or who I was with, but more importantly, about being at peace with myself and being happy rather than angry. The greatest gift my personal development journey has given me, which I once never thought possible, was finding peace in my heart and no longer being angry all the time. I imagined myself as a public speaker, perhaps as a mentor making a difference in the world. Even while I struggled with health and weight issues, I saw myself as fit, strong, and confident. So, it's no surprise that I would become a Mindset Mastery Life Coach, committed to my personal health and wellness, and overcome my fear of working out at a local gym. So, ask yourself: What are you doing today that your future self will thank you for?

Case Story: <u>Achieving the Impossible Through Love for Family</u>

John always dreamed of achieving beyond his wildest ambitions. As a dedicated family man and successful businessman, he excelled in his career but wanted to make a significant impact through charitable contributions. Fueled by love for his family and grandchildren, he set ambitious business goals and increased his charitable activities.

Though he initially saw progress, he faced numerous challenges and setbacks that were often overwhelming. Skepticism from peers made it harder, but John refused to settle for less. He focused on creating a legacy for his family and making a meaningful difference in the world.

Using each setback as a learning experience, John continued to innovate and seek new opportunities for growth.

The Path Ahead

Gradually, his business flourished, and his charitable contributions made a significant impact. His perseverance paid off, and he achieved a level of success and fulfillment he had once thought was out of reach.

John's story is a testament to the power of big dreams and the love for family as a driving force. Through determination and resilience, he not only achieved his business goals but also created a legacy of generosity and impact that will be remembered for generations.

Where Is Your Focus?

Life has a peculiar way of hiding answers, revealing them only to those who seek them. Those who have clear reasons for their actions are the ones who find the answers. As mentioned earlier in this book, "what you focus on is what you get." When you know what you want and desire it strongly, you will find ways to achieve it—where there is a will, there is a way. The answers, methods, and solutions will become evident once you have a clear "why." The necessity of finding answers drives us. Therefore, focus on the reasons first, and the answers will follow.

There are two ways to face the future: with apprehension or with anticipation. If you face it with apprehension, it is because your future isn't well-designed. Without intentional planning, you are likely to follow someone else's views of how to live. Intentional planning comes with making well-defined goals that act like a magnet, pulling you in their direction. The more clearly you define and describe your goals, the stronger their pull. They will help you overcome difficulties. Believe me, I've been there. Without goals, it's easy to let life deteriorate, to get trapped by economic necessity, and to settle for existence rather than substance. We all have a choice: we can either make a living or design a life. Deep down, we all know that there is a big dream that we want to fulfill.

Discover Your Why

Simon Sinek is a leadership expert and author best known for his book *Start With Why*. His book explores how leaders can inspire and drive success by focusing on their core purpose, emphasizing the importance of starting with the end in mind. Understanding your "why" is crucial to achieving your goals, as it serves as the foundation of your motivation and direction. It gives you a clear sense of purpose and helps you stay focused, even when challenges arise. Knowing your "why" fuels your passion and determination, making it easier to overcome obstacles and stay committed to your goals. There are various "whys" that drive and motivate individuals to achieve their goals, and it varies from person to person. I wonder what motivates you.

Family can be a major motivator. For instance, look at John's story earlier in this chapter; leaving a long-lasting legacy for his family was a significant driving force for him.

The Path Ahead

I have a friend who wanted to provide his parents with experiences they missed out on due to financial restraints, so he worked hard to become a successful business owner. Another friend of mine, a single mom, wanted to ensure a financially stable future for her two children. She became a successful entrepreneur by auctioning her artwork, selling granola, and creating an online health and wellbeing business.

Some people seek success for recognition, while others do it for the feeling of being a winner. Many constantly strive for more, not out of need, but because they enjoy the journey of winning and what it takes to get there. The wealthy and rich who continue to seek other avenues of making money often find that money is not their primary motivator; it's the journey itself and who they become in the process.

Others find motivation in considering what their success can mean for others. It's part of human nature to be driven by reasons beyond personal gain. Some people perform better for the sake of others than they do for themselves. Showing kindness, generosity, or the desire to share can be powerful motivators. Some individuals excel at accumulating resources so they can become benefactors.

A well-known example is Andrew Carnegie, a Scottish-American industrialist and philanthropist who became one of the wealthiest men of his time through his steel empire.

Goals

When Carnegie died, a slip of paper was found in one of his desk drawers with a goal he had written in his twenties: "I'm going to spend the first half of my life accumulating money, and I'm going to spend the last half of my life giving it all away." Inspired by that goal, he accumulated $450 million in the first half of his life and gave it all away in the second half to support education, libraries, and various social causes.

Goal Setting For Success

What turns you on?
What gets you up early and keeps you up late?
What inspires you?
Conversely, what turns you off?

Imagine trying to reach a destination with the wrong map—that's what it's like without clearly written goals and a plan to achieve them. With defined goals, your self-confidence and courage increase because they allow you to understand the exact steps required to achieve your dreams and make changes in your life. And as you complete each goal, it will propel you closer to your big dream of a future, providing an astonishing sense of accomplishment and purpose. And remember, it is important to celebrate each win, no matter how big or small.

Have you ever struggled to achieve a goal, repeating the same attempts without success? Perhaps you took the scenic route when a shortcut existed, or maybe you weren't aware of a more efficient method. Clearly written goals act as a compass, guiding you away from common pitfalls and steering you toward success, sparing you the disappointment, overwhelm, and anxiety that many encounter.

According to Brian Tracy's book *Goals,* fewer than 3% of people have clear, written goals and a plan for achieving them. Let's strive to be part of that 3%, especially if you're serious about making meaningful changes in your life. It's not just about jotting down vague ideas; it's about vividly envisioning your goal—what it looks like, sounds like, and feels like.

As Bob Proctor from *The Secret* says, "If you can see it in your mind, then you can see it in your hand." Clarity is key to goal attainment, and it all starts in the mind. By focusing on the details of your future, understanding what achieving those goals will provide, and aligning them with your long-term vision, you'll channel more energy and attention into that area of your life.

Setting Up The Right Mindset For Achieving Your Goals

In the outback of Australia, where the landscape is barren and traffic is sparse, it's surprising how many car accidents occur due to collisions with poles or trees.

Goals

This happens because when drivers focus too much on the obstacle they're trying to avoid, they are more likely to hit it. Our minds pay attention to whatever we focus on. Metaphorically, this applies to your journey in reaching your goals. Imagine how John's marriage and life would have been if he had let the resistance he experienced from his family get in the way. Instead, John focused on his goal and why it was important to him.

Obstacles are inevitable on the path to achieving our goals. If we don't experience challenges along the way, we might not be striving hard enough. The key is to focus on the goal itself and what achieving that goal will bring to your life. Think of how much better your life will be when you reach it. If you focus too much on the challenges or obstacles, you are more likely to get bogged down by them and settle for less.

By knowing precisely what your goal is, you gain a clear awareness of where to concentrate your efforts. Focus on the result, not the hurdles along the way. This mindset shift will help you navigate challenges more effectively and stay committed to your aspirations, dreams, and desires.

When challenges arise, or when we become too complacent, we can easily make excuses to feel better. This often happens when the journey becomes tougher, or we reach a plateau and don't see further progress. We start to rationalize our success to avoid the feeling of failure or disappointment. You tell yourself you've done pretty well, or that you're happy to have completed part of the goal and decide you don't need all of it, or that it's okay as it is.

We do this all the time. For example, if a relationship doesn't work out, you might rationalize it by saying, "She wasn't that great after all." Or if the job promotion you hoped for doesn't come through, you might say, "I didn't really want that promotion anyway because I'd be expected to do more." Or if you wanted to save for a holiday but hadn't saved the expected funds, you then say, "There is plenty of time to go on holiday," or "My job is expecting me to do overtime, so I don't have time for holidays."

The problem with these rationalizations is that we start to trade in our dreams and allow ourselves to play small. Each time we do this, we suppress ourselves and strip away a little bit of our self-worth. We rationalize to avoid the pain of being judged or to avoid the fear of not being good enough.

Sharon Pearson, the founder of The Coaching Institute of Melbourne, Australia, says in her book *Your Success,* "We take a few steps, get results, notice a plateau, and then the going gets a little tough… and the rationalizing starts again." By focusing on the positive outcomes and keeping your eyes on the prize, you can push through the challenges and achieve your goals. But now that you have this new realization of what you can focus on, you can say, "Okay, I am getting to the point of pain that I want to avoid, and I need to keep moving through this feeling."

Goals

This is when Plan B must come into play. Sharon mentions that when the tough gets tougher, we need to step into Plan B. Plan B is simple: when you hit the plateau, you raise your standards. You push through harder than usual, ask more of yourself, and don't settle for mediocre but step up instead. Remember, you are focusing on stepping up and raising your standards, not on why you are plateauing, because we now know that we need to focus on what we want, not what we don't want.

In NLP, there is no such thing as failure, only feedback, so the setback is telling you something. Think of it like a recipe for a cake: if the cake fails, what is the feedback? Was it the temperature of the oven or the measurements of the ingredients? Did you have the right ingredients, or were the ingredients put into the mixing bowl in the right order? Think of your journey toward your goal in the same way. When there is a setback or a failing moment, think about what needs to be done differently and what you need to change to get a different result. Do you think the Wright brothers got it right the first time when they wanted to invent manned flight? Or do you think NASA got it right the first time when they designed a space shuttle? They learned from their failures to succeed.

Success is failing many times and then getting back up and trying again! Think of the time you were a baby and learned to talk and walk—it took some time to fail in order to succeed. So, let's quickly look at some examples of goals versus challenges.

Example 1

Dante, a dedicated businessman, realized that his relationship with his spouse was growing distant due to his demanding work schedule. Determined to improve communication and strengthen their marriage, he set a goal to spend more quality time with his spouse. However, the challenge was finding time for meaningful conversations amidst the hectic pace of his career. Despite this, Dante made a conscious effort to prioritize his marriage, setting aside specific times each week to connect and communicate, ultimately bringing them closer together.

Example 2

Renan aspired to achieve a promotion at his company to provide better financial stability for his family. He knew that this advancement would require significant effort and increased responsibilities. The major challenge was balancing the demanding workload while ensuring he didn't neglect family time. Renan managed this by creating a structured schedule, dedicating focused time to work, and setting aside uninterrupted family time, which allowed him to succeed professionally without sacrificing his time with his family.

Example 3

Mark, a successful businessman with a busy lifestyle, aimed to lead a healthier lifestyle by exercising regularly and eating better. He faced the challenge of overcoming the temptation to skip workouts and indulge in unhealthy food due to stress and lack of time. To tackle this, Mark integrated short, effective workouts into his daily routine and planned healthy meals in advance, gradually adopting a more balanced lifestyle that enhanced his well-being and set a positive example for his family.

Be SMART About Your Goals

The S.M.A.R.T. model is a powerful framework for setting and achieving objectives effectively. This method ensures that your goals are clearly defined and realistic, with a way to track progress and a deadline to help maintain focus. By applying the S.M.A.R.T. criteria, you can transform vague aspirations into actionable plans, increasing your chances of success and making it easier to stay motivated and organized.

S – Specific: A specific goal is clearly defined and unambiguous. To set a specific goal, answer the five "W" questions: Who is involved? What do I want to accomplish? Where will it happen? When do I want to achieve it? Why is this goal important? Being specific helps to focus your efforts and set clear, actionable steps toward achieving your objective.

For example, instead of saying "I want to get fit," a specific goal would be "I want to run a 5K race by October 1st."

- **Who:** Who is involved?

- **What:** What do I want to accomplish?

- **Where:** Identify a location.

- **When:** Establish a time frame.

- **Which:** Identify requirements and constraints.

- **Why:** Specific reasons, purpose, or benefits of accomplishing the goal.

-

M – Measurable: You need clear evidence to know when you have reached your goal. This evidence could be a specific weight, a number of clients, a distance to run, or a certain amount of money in the bank. Determine the metrics that will track your progress, including any relevant dates and quantities. Measuring your progress helps you stay on track, meet target dates, and experience the satisfaction of achievement, motivating you to continue your efforts toward reaching your goal.

A – Attainable: An attainable goal is one that is achievable. When you identify goals that are most important to you, you start figuring out ways to make them happen. You develop the necessary attitudes, abilities, skills, and financial capacity to reach them. This focus helps you recognize previously overlooked opportunities that can bring you closer to achieving your goals.

Goals

R – Realistic: A realistic goal is within reach but still requires effort and determination. To be realistic, a goal must represent an objective you are both willing and able to work toward. Goals can be both high and realistic; only you can decide how ambitious your goal should be. Ensure that each goal represents substantial progress. Interestingly, high goals often motivate more than low ones, as they push you to exert more effort. Sometimes, the most challenging tasks feel easier when they are driven by passion and love.

T – Time-bound: A goal should be grounded within a specific timeframe to create a sense of urgency. Without a set date, there's no pressure to take action. For example, if you want to lose 10 lbs, specifying "one day" or "next month" won't work because it lacks commitment. However, if you set a specific deadline, like "by May 1st," it activates your unconscious mind to start working toward the goal. Using significant dates, such as anniversaries or birthdays, can also provide additional motivation and focus.

Looking at the three examples of goals mentioned earlier with Dante, Renan, and Mark, let's now put them in the format of using the SMART model as shown below.

Example 1 - Dante's Goal (S.M.A.R.T. Format):

- **Specific:** Dante aims to improve communication and strengthen his marriage by spending more quality time with his spouse.

- **Measurable:** Dante will spend at least 3 hours per week in meaningful conversations with his spouse.

- **Achievable:** By setting aside specific times each week, Dante can manage his schedule to include quality time with his spouse.

- **Relevant:** Improving his marriage is important to Dante, as he values a strong, communicative relationship with his spouse.

- **Time-bound:** Dante will implement this plan over the next three months and evaluate the improvement in their relationship.

-

Example 2 - Renan's Goal (S.M.A.R.T. Format):

- **Specific:** Renan aims to achieve a promotion at his company to provide better financial stability for his family.

- **Measurable:** Renan will dedicate an extra 10 hours per week to his work responsibilities while ensuring he spends at least 15 hours of uninterrupted time with his family each week.

- **Achievable:** By creating a structured schedule, Renan can balance his increased workload and family time.

- **Relevant:** Achieving a promotion is crucial for Renan's goal of providing better financial stability for his family.
- **Time-bound:** Renan will follow this structured schedule for the next six months and review his progress towards the promotion and work-life balance.

Example 3 - Alex's Goal (S.M.A.R.T. Format):

- **Specific:** Alex aims to lead a healthier lifestyle by exercising regularly and eating better.
- **Measurable:** Alex will exercise for at least 30 minutes, five times a week, and plan healthy meals every Sunday for the upcoming week.
- **Achievable:** By integrating short, effective workouts into his routine and planning meals in advance, Alex can overcome his busy lifestyle's challenges.
- **Relevant:** Leading a healthier lifestyle is essential for Alex's well-being and setting a positive example for his family.
- **Time-bound:** Alex will follow this plan for the next three months and assess the improvement in his health and well-being.

Make a List

Unhappiness often comes from within, regardless of how good our external circumstances might be. You might have plenty of money, a nice home, and food on the table, but still feel unfulfilled. Some people, no matter how much they have, are always dissatisfied and complain about every little thing. This inner turmoil usually stems from being unhappy with oneself. To break free from this, recognize and address any limiting beliefs or negative philosophies holding you back. Start by creating a list of goals and reasons that inspire you. Yes, setbacks will happen, but with a compelling reason to drive you, you'll find the motivation to pursue something truly unique. Speaking from personal experience, this mindset can lead to meaningful change.

Your list can include anything from the seemingly trivial to the deeply personal. Decide what you want and write it down. It's that simple. Think about the ordinary or even silly things you'd like to do. For instance, I heard a story on a podcast about a Chinese man who humorously listed a goal of having a Caucasian gardener. This reminds us that goals can be anything, no matter how unusual they seem.

Goals can be small and easy, contributing to the bigger picture. Three years ago, I set a small goal to switch from full cream milk to almond milk and from caffeinated to decaf coffee. These small changes aligned with my larger goal of becoming a fit and strong motivational speaker.

Goals

As you create your list, think about the small joys you'd experience, like proving your critics wrong or the satisfaction of meeting your responsibilities and helping others. Gather your loved ones—family, friends, colleagues—and make a list together. Setting ambitious goals, like becoming a millionaire, isn't just about the money; it's about who you become in the process. Imagine how many people you could help or what charities you could support.

Aim for goals that challenge and stretch you, pushing you to grow beyond your current self. Live at the summit. Embrace challenges and go where the demands are high and expectations stretch you to your limits.

Consider these questions:

- **Where do you want to go?**
- **What do you want to do?**
- **What do you want to share?**
- **What projects do you want to support?**
- **What do you want to be known for?**
- **Who do you want to see?**
- **What very important things do you want to do?**
- **What do you want to have?**
- **What skills do you want to learn?**
- **Who do you want to be?**
- **Who are you becoming here?**

Remember, it's who you become that makes you valuable. Set goals that will make something of you in the process of achieving them. What will they make of you? Don't set your goals too low. Don't join an easy crowd where you won't grow. Instead, go where expectations and demands are high.

Over the next five years, focus on growth and change. Commit to not remaining the same. Avoid compromise and never sell out. Now that we've explored your identity, values, and beliefs, and you have a greater awareness of your strengths and where you want to go, it's time to start writing out your goals. These goals will serve as stepping stones to the future you desire.

One Goal at a Time: Avoiding the Trap of Goal Overload

Instead of spreading yourself thin by focusing on several goals at once, concentrate on one goal—the most important one right now. Let's take a closer look at your goals and prioritize them so you can focus your time and effort on what matters most. Effective goal setting is not just about identifying what you want but also recognizing what you must give up to achieve it. Many people are unwilling to make the conscious decision to let go of certain things in their life to reach their goals.

The more success and achievement we attain, the bigger the challenges we face.

Goals

With greater success, there is more at risk and more to lose, but this is a positive sign—it means we have stepped up. Embrace these challenges, as they guide us and make us stronger for what lies ahead.

Write down five goals using the table below:

1. Attribute: Base one goal on an attribute or a character quality that you desire to develop within yourself.
2. Activity: Set one goal for something you want to do.
3. Possession: Select one goal for something you want to have.
4. Open: The last two goals can be whatever you choose.

Include with your goals the reasons why you will achieve each goal within the next twelve months. Remember, it is when we have a compelling reason why that we find the motivation to move forward.

Your Goals:

- Goal One:

- Goal Two:

- Goal Three:

- Goal Four:

- Goal Five:

Conclusion

In this chapter, we've explored the powerful role that dreaming big and setting meaningful goals play in shaping your future. Goal-setting isn't just about creating a list of things to achieve—it's about connecting deeply with your "why" and using that connection to fuel your daily actions.

Dreaming big gives your goals purpose, transforming them from mere ambitions into a driving force that helps you navigate obstacles. When aligned with your core desires and values, your goals become a compass guiding you toward personal growth and fulfillment. Through perseverance and resilience, you can overcome setbacks and stay on course, learning as much from the journey as the destination.

The S.M.A.R.T. framework offers a practical way to turn your dreams into reality by providing clarity and focus. But remember, it's not just about achieving goals; it's about who you become along the way. Each step you take toward your dreams shapes your character and builds the life you truly want.

As you move forward, keep dreaming boldly and stay intentional in your actions. Your goals are a map, but visualization is the tool that will bring those dreams into sharp focus. In the final chapter, we'll explore how to use the power of visualization to turn your aspirations into tangible reality, connecting your inner vision with external success.

Chapter Ten

Visualizing

A Journey to Fearless Living

"The punishment of desire is the agony of unfulfillment."

- *Hermes Trismegistus*

The Path to Your Ideal Life

Now that you have developed a stronger sense of self, a healthier self-image, and a renewed level of self-belief, your goals may look entirely different from where they were at the beginning of this journey. This newfound confidence and belief in yourself might feel unfamiliar, but it is the key to unlocking the life you truly desire.

In the previous chapter, we explored the power of setting goals and dreaming big. Having big dreams is the first step toward creating a life of purpose and fulfillment, but it's important to understand that dreams alone aren't enough.

Visualization is the tool that transforms those dreams into a clear and actionable vision.

While dreams inspire us to imagine what could be, visualization allows us to map out the steps to get there, making the abstract tangible and the impossible achievable. As we conclude this journey, it is with great joy and satisfaction that I now share with you the powerful practice of visualization. This is a tool I regularly use to shape the outcomes of my day, week, month, season, or year. Whether I'm preparing for speaking events or the kapa haka performances I occasionally participate in, visualization plays a crucial role. This practice helped me land my perfect job on the Sun Princess, guiding me away from being stuck in a traditional 9-to-5 job.

Instead, it opened avenues for me to earn more while working less, often getting paid to travel, and allowing me to live in a beautiful part of Sydney. Visualization has been my guiding light through both the successes and challenges in my life.

Here are three reasons why I have saved this extremely valuable tool for the final chapter:

1. **Recognize the Power Within You:** By visualizing your future, you unlock the doors to a life of unparalleled fulfillment, recognizing the extraordinary power that lies within you. Visualization is more than daydreaming; it is an intentional practice that can reshape your reality.

2. **Embrace a Vivid Picture of Your Future:** Visualization allows you to embrace a way of thinking that paints a clear and vibrant picture of your ideal life. This mental image serves as a beacon, guiding you toward your goals and dreams.

3. **Liberate Yourself and Catalyze Transformation:** Visualization liberates you from the limitations imposed by societal norms and expectations. It acts as a catalyst for incredible transformation, allowing you to break free from conventional constraints, pursue your authentic path, and open possibilities that once seemed out of reach.

The Power of Visualization

Your ideal future and desired outcomes gives the Reticular Activating System (RAS) in your brain something to focus on. As we discussed in an earlier chapter, the RAS plays a crucial role in filtering information and bringing relevant details to your attention. By vividly visualizing your future, you prime your RAS to seek out anything related to your ideal future, making you extra aware of opportunities and ensuring you pay attention to what truly matters.

Dr. Joe Dispenza, a renowned expert in the field, teaches that visualization is the key to unlocking your most incredible, rich, and ideal life. It allows you to see and feel your future self-living the life you dream of, setting the stage for actualizing these dreams.

We will also draw upon the works of Dr. Wayne Dyer, an internationally renowned author and speaker in the field of self-development, who emphasizes the profound impact of visualization on personal growth and fulfillment. Dr. Dyer teaches that visualization can transform your life by aligning your thoughts and actions with your highest aspirations. His insights will further illuminate the path to harnessing the power of your imagination to create the life you envision.

This chapter will guide you through the steps to harness the power of visualization, ensuring you leave this book not only inspired but equipped with the tools to transform your aspirations into reality. Let's embark on this final step together, imagining the extraordinary life that awaits you.

Believe It, Then See It

In the introduction of this book, I shared how I visualized in my mind what it would feel like to work for Princess Cruises before I was accepted for the job and offered the Assistant Cruise Director position. I vividly imagined myself walking the outer decks of the ship, feeling the sun on my skin, and smelling the sea breeze. I felt a deep sense of pride and told myself, "I did it."

This powerful belief in my vision set the wheels in motion. Before I knew it, I was there, walking the outer deck in the sun on one of the Princess Cruises ships.

Visualizing

I had reached my goal because I believed in the power of my thoughts and feelings. By focusing on a clear and positive vision of what I wanted, and truly believing it was possible, I was able to attract that reality into my life. This is the essence of what Drs. Joe Dispenza and Wayne Dyer teach: our thoughts and emotions shape our experiences.

When we imagine our dreams vividly and feel as if they have already come true, we set the stage for them to manifest in our reality. The key is not just to visualize but to truly believe in the outcome you desire. A person with a scarcity mindset cannot experience abundance. We don't see the world as it is; we see it as we are. It's our choice! To see something first and then believe in it requires imagination, but to believe first and then see it, requires conviction.

Imagine what your life could be like if you had no limitations— what would you do? Life unfolds in fascinating ways, and the universe works in accordance with our thoughts, creating the frequency and energy to attract what we think about.

The RAS makes anything important to us stand out like never before. When we believe in our vision and pay attention, we notice that people, conversations, books, Uber rides, and even bus delays have something important to share. Whenever something unfortunate, like a cancelled flight or a missed bus occurs, I often think,

"There is something wonderful about to happen; I am about to receive information that is important to me." Give it a try—believe in the positive outcome, say it, and take note throughout the day of what happens. It's as if we are the creators of our own reality.

The Crucial Role of Self-Talk

In the process of visualization, the way you talk to yourself plays a vital role in shaping your reality. Dr. Dyer emphasized this in his book *Your Erroneous Zones*. He suggests that you can do whatever you want simply because you want to, and for no other reason. This empowering mindset can open new vistas of experience and help eliminate the fear of the unknown that might otherwise hold you back.

As we mentioned earlier in chapter Eight: *Language: Rewriting Your Narrative for Success*, our thoughts form our feelings and emotions. In essence, how we talk to ourselves directly influences how we feel and, consequently, how we act. This is why it's crucial to pair positive self-talk with your visualization practice. When you visualize your goals or ideal future, infusing that mental image with positive, encouraging self-talk can amplify your emotional connection to the vision, making it feel more real and achievable.

During my time working on the Sun Princess, I made it a habit to celebrate even the small victories. Navigating the ship's many corridors and hidden passageways,

Visualizing

I would often give myself a mental high five, praising myself for taking the risk to apply for the job. It would have been easy to succumb to self-doubt, but instead, I chose to reinforce my belief in myself. This habit of self-celebration became essential to maintaining my stamina, motivation, drive, and overall well-being. The sooner you embrace the power of positive self-talk, the sooner you'll start seeing more favourable results in your life.

Harnessing the Practise of Visualization

Visualizing your ideal future or desired outcome is taking the use of your imagination to a whole new level. Visualizing your goals effectively can create an incredible shift in your life.

You can make current decisions based on the image of your vision to determine if your choices are productive, resourceful, and helping you move toward your ideal future. It also allows you to see if your choices are wasteful, unresourceful, and moving you away from your ideal outcome. Picture this new approach of visualization as a roadmap to peel away the layers of doubt and self-limiting beliefs. Allow your true self to emerge. During a visualization exercise or meditation, allow yourself to feel the emotions and savour the moments associated with the imagery. Then notice your self-talk—is it one of encouragement, appreciation, or perhaps even love? It can be whatever you choose it to be.

The more vivid and realistic your visualization, the more your mind will connect with the process, making it easier to stay focused and committed. This deep engagement with the visualization process helps to anchor your intentions, making the journey toward your goal more tangible and achievable.

Effective Visualization: Two Key Aspects

1. Goal Visualization

This involves picturing a future outcome that you are committed to making real and applying true feelings and emotions to that picture. Consider how you will know when you have reached that goal. What is the language of your self-talk? What would the sense of accomplishment feel like? Consider what the feelings of success would feel like. What are the tangible signs or evidence that show you have reached that success? How are you feeling in the visualization? The picture needs to include something you can measure, hold, or see. In Dr. Dispenza's impactful presentations, such as *"Shift Your Emotions and Transform Your Life,"* he delves into the concept that the mind lacks the ability to distinguish between reality and imagination. He advocates for creating a vivid mental image of our desired future, coupled with the corresponding emotions. These fusion tricks the body into believing that the envisioned success is already a present reality.

Is there a certain balance in your bank account? Maybe it's witnessing the birth of your first child or attending your children's graduation. Perhaps you are struggling with anger management or addictions, and your ideal future involves being happier and living a sober life. Your ideal end goal could be you standing in front of a community dealing with the same issues you have overcome, sharing your success story with them.

2. Process Visualization

Unlike goal visualization, where you focus on the end picture of your goal, process visualization involves picturing yourself running through the steps and processes taken to achieve the vision of your end goal. It's helpful to break down the journey into smaller, manageable milestones. Visualize each step you need to take, no matter how small, and see yourself successfully completing each one. This approach not only makes the overall goal less overwhelming but also provides a sense of accomplishment as you progress, reinforcing your motivation and confidence along the way.

Addressing Common Obstacles in Visualization

As powerful as visualization can be, it's not uncommon to encounter challenges along the way. Here are some common obstacles people face when trying to visualize and strategies to overcome them:

1. **Negative Self-Talk:** One of the biggest barriers to effective visualization is negative self-talk. This inner critic can undermine your confidence and disrupt the clarity of your vision. To counteract this, it's crucial to consciously replace negative thoughts with positive affirmations. Whenever doubt creeps in, remind yourself of your strengths and past successes. Visualize not only your goals but also the positive self-talk that will accompany your journey toward achieving them. The more you practice this, the stronger your belief in your own potential will become.

2. **Difficulty Maintaining Focus:** Maintaining focus during visualization can be challenging, especially in a world full of distractions. If you find your mind wandering during visualization exercises, start with shorter sessions and gradually increase the length as your focus improves. Practicing mindfulness techniques, such as deep breathing or guided meditation, can also help enhance your concentration. Creating a quiet, dedicated space for visualization can further minimize distractions and improve your ability to stay focused on your vision.

3. **Overcoming Scepticism:** You might wonder if visualization really works or if it's just wishful thinking. To overcome this, start by experimenting with visualization on smaller, more attainable goals. As you begin to see results, your confidence in the process will grow. Remember that visualization is not about magically manifesting results without effort; it's about aligning your mindset and actions with your desired outcomes.

Keeping a journal to track your progress can help reinforce your belief in the power of visualization as you observe the positive changes it brings to your life. By recognizing and addressing these obstacles, you can enhance your visualization practice and make it a more effective tool for achieving your goals. Visualization, when practiced with persistence and belief, can become a powerful ally in your journey toward personal and professional fulfillment.

The Power of Immersive Visualization

Research suggests that by vividly picturing the life we desire and infusing it with genuine emotions associated with that vision, we initiate a transformative process that extends far beyond mere wishful thinking. Enhance your process visualization by incorporating as many sensory details and emotions as possible. Imagine what each step will look, sound, feel, taste and even smell like.

You need to build yourself with affirmations that positively reinforce the attainment of the visualization. This strengthens your belief in your ability to do what is required to achieve it. This is crucial because many people fail to achieve their goals due to a lack of self-belief. Focus on the journey, not just the destination.

Are there rituals you have in place or a community that champions you?

If You Don't Know What You Want, You Will Never Get It

By envisioning your desired future vividly and with intention, you create a mental blueprint that your mind and body can follow. Clarity is the foundation of all achievement. Yet, it fascinates me, though it never surprises me, that so many of my clients, friends, and family struggle to articulate what they truly want in life. For many, this becomes new territory—thinking about desires and goals with precision and specificity. Instead, they often become adept at identifying and expressing what they don't want.

To move beyond this barrier:

- **You need to be clear about where in life you wish to be.** Clarity in your destination is crucial because it sets the direction for all your efforts and decisions.

- **You must have a clear understanding of the characteristics required to go on such a mission with your vision.** Identifying the skills, mindset, and resources needed will prepare you for the journey ahead.

- **What would the emotions and feelings be like once you are living that vision? Can you live in that moment now as if it were already here?** Connecting emotionally with your vision helps to solidify it in your mind and drives your commitment to achieving it.

Dr. Joe Dispenza emphasizes the crucial role of envisioning our future, placing it at the forefront of his teachings. His insights shed light on a powerful truth: our minds possess an extraordinary ability to shape our reality. Imagine this journey as creating a vision board for your life, allowing you to design the future you dream of for yourself and those you hold dear to.

The Heart-Brain Connection

The intricate network of cells within our bodies functions as conduits for light and information, generating a potent energy that vibrates at a certain frequency—the higher, the better.

When this energy is harnessed and regulated effectively, it can fortify our immune system, optimize digestive functions, and keep our minds sharp. Dr. Dispenza emphasizes the profound symbiotic relationship between our mental states and physiological well-being, particularly highlighting how our hearts and brains communicate and influence each other. He asserts that our bodies respond to the renewal of our minds and hearts as if these transformations were organically unfolding from within.

Rather than attempting to manipulate external circumstances, Dr. Dispenza underscores the significance of internal transformation. He posits that striving to alter the tangible aspects of our lives without first changing ourselves leads to prolonged efforts and delayed manifestations of our desires. The scientific evidence supporting this perspective extends to the intricate interplay between the heart, brain, and gene expression, as well as the dynamic energy emitted by individuals and amplified within a group setting.

In the realm of Te Matatini Kapa Haka competitions, the unity and combined power of 40 performers moving as one is a profound expression of *kotahitanga*—the concept of collective unity. This collective energy is a perfect example of the heart-brain connection at work on a larger scale. When every member of the group aligns their hearts and minds, focusing their energy, thoughts, and intentions harmoniously, the impact is palpable. This shared focus creates a powerful, coherent, and transformative environment that resonates not only within the group but also with the audience. The *wairua* (spirit) of the performance is elevated, demonstrating the immense strength that comes from a collective united in purpose.

This unity of heart and mind among performers is a living example of how interconnected our mental and physiological states are, and how this connection can create profound, transformative experiences.

The Science of Repetition

In our lives, a single occurrence is often labelled an incident, a repeat event is considered a coincidence, and when patterns emerge, we recognize a trend. This repetitive nature, when observable and consistent, is the essence of science—a system of reproducible experiences. Consider the impact of an experience on someone's perspective; it has the potential to alter the way they view life. Think of this change as a formula, akin to learning a dance move or perfecting a golf swing. Initially, it's a deliberate effort, but with time and practice, it transforms into a habit or skill.

Learning, in essence, involves forging synaptic connections and developing new neurological insights. It's about creating those initial connections and then, through remembering, maintaining, and sustaining them. As understanding deepens, a person

constructs a mental model. If someone can articulate and explain a concept, they are essentially programming the neurological hardware needed to undergo that experience. The clearer we grasp the 'what' and 'why' of a situation, the 'how' naturally falls into place.

Further Reading and References

1. **Dispenza, Joe. (2012).** *Breaking the Habit of Being Yourself: How to Lose Your Mind and Create a New One.* Hay House Inc.

   o Dr. Joe Dispenza delves into the science of how our thoughts and emotions shape our reality. This book offers practical guidance on how to harness the power of visualization to create lasting change.

2. **Dyer, Wayne. (2004).** *The Power of Intention: Learning to Co-create Your World Your Way.* Hay House Inc.

   o In this transformative book, Dr. Wayne Dyer explores how intention shapes our lives. His teachings on the importance of aligning your thoughts and actions with your highest aspirations are essential for anyone looking to harness the power of visualization.

3. **Dispenza, Joe. (2017).** *Becoming Supernatural: How Common People Are Doing the Uncommon.* Hay House Inc.

   o This book further explores the connection between our thoughts, emotions, and physical health, emphasizing the role of the heart-brain

   o and how to use it to achieve extraordinary outcomes.

4. **Hill, Napoleon. (1937).** *Think and Grow Rich.* The Ralston Society.

   o A classic in the realm of personal development, Hill's book discusses the power of thought and belief in achieving financial and personal success. His insights on visualization and mindset are timeless.

5. **Proctor, Bob. (2015).** *The Art of Living.* TarcherPerigee.

   o Bob Proctor, one of the leading figures in the personal development field, offers practical advice on how to live a fulfilling life by understanding and applying the laws of the universe, including the power of visualization.

6. **Tolle, Eckhart. (2004).** *The Power of Now: A Guide to Spiritual Enlightenment.* New World Library.

   o Eckhart Tolle emphasizes the importance of living in the present moment and how this awareness can transform your approach to life and visualization.

Suggested Reading

To deepen your understanding and practice of visualization, I highly recommend exploring these resources. Each book provides valuable perspectives on how our thoughts, beliefs, and intentions shape our reality. As you read, you'll discover practical techniques and insights that can help you further align your mind, heart, and actions with the life you envision.

Suggested YouTube Resources:

Rewired Summit | 60s | 1920x1080

Dr. Joe Dispenza's Guided Meditation for Visualization: https://www.youtube.com/watch?v=Pn0VrRcG-U4

Opening The Minds Eye - Visualization

The Mind's Eye: Visualization Techniques and Guided Meditation: https://www.youtube.com/watch?v=iMj8oIbZDqU **Techniques**

Music to do your self-guided Visualization and meditation:

https://www.youtube.com/watch?v=jOT1woUVZC4 **The Heart-Brain Coherence - Real Power of Feeling and Imagination!**

Chapter Summary

In this final chapter, we explored the powerful practice of visualization and how it serves as the bridge between dreams and reality. By now, you have developed a stronger sense of self, a healthier self-image, and a renewed level of self-belief.

Visualizing

With these tools in hand, your goals and aspirations have likely evolved, becoming clearer and more aligned with your true desires.

We've delved into purpose, identity, beliefs, values, worldviews, fears, relationships, trauma, healing, and the impact of father-son relationships on the development of men. Through case stories and examples, we've seen that the desire for a fulfilling life is universal.

We delved into the mechanics of visualization, including the importance of goal and process visualization, and how engaging your senses and emotions can make your visions more vivid and achievable. We also addressed common obstacles that might arise, such as negative self-talk, difficulty maintaining focus, and scepticism, and provided strategies to overcome these challenges.

Additionally, we examined the profound connection between the heart and brain, emphasizing how internal transformation can lead to external success. Whether in the context of individual goals or collective efforts like those seen in the Te Matatini Kapa Haka competitions, the power of aligned energy and intention cannot be overstated.

Quotes and Insights

To reinforce the importance of taking action and starting where you are, consider these insightful quotes from various thought leaders:

1. **Brown, Caroline.** *"To get good at anything, you just gotta start doing it."*

   o Caroline Brown highlights the power of taking the first step, no matter how small. This simple yet profound advice serves as a reminder that progress begins with action.

2. **Wood, Claire.** *"I love that. It's more important that we begin."*

   o Claire Wood echoes the sentiment that the journey to success starts with the decision to begin. Her perspective encourages you to take that crucial first step toward your goals.

3. **Milevska, Elena.** *"Yes, that sits better with me. Small steps every day, and we'll surprise ourselves with the results."*

   o Elena Milevska emphasizes the value of consistency and incremental progress. Her words remind us that small, daily actions can lead to significant and surprising results over time.

4. **Johnson, Jason.** *"That's beautiful. I'll bring more of that into my life. Looking forward to learning more about it in the course."*

   o Jason Johnson's reflection illustrates the importance of integrating new practices into our daily lives. His eagerness to learn and apply these concepts is a testament to the power of embracing new knowledge.

Final Thoughts

We all share common ground in our experiences of wounds, struggles, grief, or trauma. These shared experiences connect us and underscore our collective journey toward living happily and loving ourselves again.

Imagine a world where men take the time to heal their own wounds, breaking the cycles of pain and trauma that have been passed down through generations. When fathers embark on this path of healing, they not only transform their own lives but also the lives of their children, creating a foundation of love, understanding, and emotional safety.

By healing themselves, fathers become more attuned to the needs of their children, nurturing their growth with empathy and wisdom. They create a space where their children feel seen, valued, and supported—where the little ones can flourish without the burden of unresolved pain. This healing also extends to their relationships with their wives or partners, fostering a connection built on mutual respect and understanding.

When a father is whole, he is better equipped to listen, to truly hear and understand the voice of his partner, allowing them to feel valued and appreciated for who they are.

In this healed state, a man no longer needs to seek validation through external measures; instead, he finds strength and fulfillment in his identity as a father, husband, and individual.

The Path Ahead

He is appreciated not for what he provides materially, but for who he is—his presence, his love, his guidance. The relationships he nurtures become a testament to the power of healing, transforming the family unit into a haven of peace and support.

As you move forward, I encourage you to embrace this vision of healing—both for yourself and for those you love. Your journey of self-discovery is not just for you; it is a gift you give to your family. By continuing to grow, to heal, and to live with intention, you set the stage for a legacy of love and understanding that will echo through the generations.

As you move forward, remember that the journey of self-discovery and growth does not end here. The insights and practices you've gained throughout this book are tools you can continue to refine and apply in your life. Visualization is not a one-time event but a continuous practice that evolves as you do. By consistently applying the principles of visualization, self-belief, and intentional action, you can create a life that reflects your deepest values and aspirations.

Visualizing

Leave a Review!

Thank you for taking the time to read *The Path Ahead: Discover Who You Are and What You Want in Life.* If you enjoyed the book and found it helpful, I would greatly appreciate it if you could leave a review on Amazon. Your feedback not only helps me as an author to improve and create better content, but it also plays a crucial role in helping other readers discover the book. Reviews are essential for spreading the word and connecting with those who might benefit from the message of *The Path Ahead.* You can share your thoughts and leave a review by visiting the review section when you type the title of this book in the search bar on Amazon.

Feel free to send us an email shall you require further information or have any enquiries at the email below: info@thepathahead.com.au

Thank you for your support!

Chapter Summaries / Endnotes / References:

Chapter One: Purpose– Navigating Your Path

In this foundational chapter, you will explore the profound importance of finding your life's purpose. Purpose is the anchor that provides direction, motivation, and meaning to your life. Through personal anecdotes, practical tools, and deep reflection, you will learn how self-awareness, authenticity, and alignment with your core values are essential steps toward living a fulfilling life. The chapter also emphasizes the evolving nature of purpose, the power of serving others, and the importance of resilience in overcoming life's obstacles. Finally, you'll discover how cultivating gratitude can strengthen your connection to your purpose and help you live a life of abundance and fulfillment.

Endnotes and References

1. Positive Psychology – Reference Martin Seligman's work on Positive Psychology and the concept of "flourishing," which aligns with the idea of living a meaningful life.

   o Suggested Reference: Seligman, M. E. P. (2011). *Flourish: A Visionary New Understanding of Happiness and Well-being.* Free Press.

2. Tony Robbins' Core Human Needs – Reference Tony Robbins' six human needs model to support the section on significance.

   o Suggested Reference: Robbins, Tony (1997). *Awaken the Giant Within: How to Take Immediate Control of Your Mental, Emotional, Physical, and Financial Destiny!*

   o Using vision boards to program the RAS aligns our focus with our goals

Chapter Two: Perspectives

In Chapter Two, "Perspective," you'll discover how your perception shapes your reality and learn how to harness this power to create meaningful change in your life. By understanding the profound impact of your thoughts and focus, you'll gain insights into how to respond to life's challenges in ways that serve you. This chapter explores the science behind your brain's filtering system, the Reticular Activating System (RAS), and reveals why where you direct your attention determines the quality of your experiences. Through practical examples and powerful concepts, you'll learn to shift your mindset, focus on solutions, and unlock your potential to live a more fulfilling and intentional life.

Endnotes

1. **Understanding Perception:**

   o Steven Covey's quote, "We don't see the world as it is, we see the world as we are," emphasizes the subjective nature of perception and its influence on our reality. Neuroscience and personal development research highlight that while external factors are often beyond our control, our responses to them are within our power.

2. **The Role of the RAS:**

   o The Reticular Activating System (RAS) filters information based on our values, beliefs, and experiences, o   shaping our internal representation of the world. By tuning into what is relevant to our thoughts and goals, the RAS helps us focus on opportunities and resources that align with our desires.

3. **Focus and Reality Creation:**

o   The principle "where attention goes, energy flows" illustrates how focused attention can amplify efforts and outcomes, fostering a more fulfilling and successful life. Mindfulness and gratitude practices can help maintain a positive focus, enhancing resilience and personal growth.

Behavioral Influence:

o   Our thoughts lead to emotions, which then influence our behaviors and actions, creating a feedback loop that reinforces our perception and reality. Changing our perspective, as demonstrated in the personal example of shifting from impatience to empathy, can immediately alter our emotional state and reactions.

4. **Practical Applications:**

o   Using vision boards to program the RAS aligns our focus with our goals, making us more aware of daily opportunities to achieve them. Asking reflective questions can expand our awareness and to help us find solutions outside of our current thinking patterns.

1. Reticular Activating System (RAS) and Focus

- **Research:** The Reticular Activating System (RAS) is a network of neurons located in the brainstem, and its primary role is to regulate arousal and consciousness, filtering sensory information and allowing selective focus.

    o Source: Vanderah, T.W., & Gould, D.J. (2016). *Nolte's The Human Brain: An Introduction to Its Functional Anatomy.* This textbook provides foundational neuroscience insights into the RAS.

    o Application: Including a scientific explanation of how the RAS works will bolster your discussion on how focus shapes perception and how it filters out unnecessary information to highlight what we deem important.

2. Law of Attraction and Positive Thinking

- Research: The Law of Attraction is rooted in the idea that our thoughts attract experiences, as discussed by Bob Proctor in personal development and success coaching.

    o Source: Proctor, B. (1984). *You Were Born Rich.* This book provides an in-depth exploration of the Law of Attraction and how thoughts influence outcomes.

    o   Application: Cite Proctor's works as a resource to support your argument that "like attracts like" and that shifting focus toward solutions attracts more solutions.

3. Cognitive Behavioral Therapy (CBT) and Thought Patterns

- Research: Cognitive Behavioral Therapy (CBT) shows that changing one's thoughts can directly affect emotions and behaviors, aligning with your idea of reframing perception to change outcomes.

    o   Source: Beck, A.T. (1976). *Cognitive Therapy and the Emotional Disorders.* explains how perception and thought patterns influence emotional experiences.

    o   Application: Incorporating this research will add psychological credibility to the claim that shifting thoughts can transform one's emotional and behavioral reality.

4. Carl Jung's Analytical Psychology and Perception

- Research: Carl Jung's work on the collective unconscious and personal projections aligns with your mention of "we don't see things as they are, but as we are."

    o   Source: Jung, C.G. (1968). *Man and His Symbols.* This book explores Jung's ideas on perception, projection, and the human psyche.

    o   Application: This research will add depth to your discussion on how self-perception influences our interpretation of reality and experiences.

5. Mindfulness and Neuroplasticity

- Research: Mindfulness practices help train the brain to focus attention purposefully, and research in neuroplasticity demonstrates that the brain changes in response to where we place our focus.

  - Source: Davidson, R.J., & Goleman, D. (2017). *Altered Traits: Science Reveals How Meditation Changes Your Mind, Brain, and Body.* This book provides empirical evidence of how mindfulness practices reshape the brain.

  - Application: Cite this research to reinforce your discussion on how mindfulness and focusing on positive outcomes rewires the brain to help create desired reality.

6. Viktor Frankl's Logotherapy and Meaning

- Research: Viktor Frankl's logotherapy emphasizes finding meaning in life's events, which is closely related to your point about changing perception to alter emotional responses.

  - Source: Frankl, V.E. (2006). *Man's Search for Meaning.* This classic work discusses how individuals can find meaning and reshape their perspective.

  - Application: This reference supports the idea that we can shift our perception, even in adversity, to find meaning and improve our emotional experience.

7. Positive Psychology and Gratitude

- Research: Studies in positive psychology have shown that focusing on gratitude can shift our emotional state and reduce feelings of fear and anxiety.

Chapter Summaries / Endnotes / References:

- ○ Source: Emmons, R.A., & McCullough, M.E. (2003). *Counting Blessings Versus Burdens: An Experimental Investigation of Gratitude and Subjective Well-Being in Daily Life.* This research demonstrates how practicing gratitude improves mental health and shifts perceptions.

- ○ Application: Including this research will support your discussion on how gratitude can shift focus from fear to appreciation, thereby improving emotional well-being.

Chapter Three: Identity

In Chapter Three, we explore the profound concept of identity and how it influences every aspect of your life. Understanding your true self is essential for living authentically, fostering emotional well-being, and achieving your goals. The chapter delves into the importance of aligning your self-perception with your core identity and the role of beliefs and values in shaping who you are. This chapter explores how your self-perception, often shaped by how you believe others see you, impacts your fulfillment, emphasizing the importance of embracing your authentic self. It addresses how limiting beliefs, rooted in past experiences, can hinder your potential, and offers strategies to challenge and replace them for a more empowered mindset. Understanding and aligning with your core values is highlighted as essential for leading a purposeful life. The chapter also introduces Māori concepts such as whakapapa (genealogy) and kaitiakitanga (guardianship), stressing the significance of connection to ancestry, community, and nature in shaping identity. Practical tools, including self-reflection questions, journaling prompts, and activities, are provided to help you build a stronger sense of self.

The Path Ahead

Endnotes

1. **Exploring Identity:**

   o Identity is shaped by self-perception, beliefs, and values, influencing decision-making and life satisfaction.

   o Authentic living leads to smoother experiences and helps overcome negative habits and emotional challenges.

2. **The Influence of Beliefs:**

   o Charles Cooley's perspective highlights that self-perception is often influenced by how we believe others perceive us, leading to feelings of inadequacy and impostor syndrome.

   o Brian Tracy emphasizes that negative emotions stem from fear of loss, rejection, or criticism. Improving self-image and self-esteem helps overcome these emotions.

3. **Self-Perception and Self-Esteem:**

   o Self-perception, shaped by past experiences, can create an imagined self rather than the true self.

   o Building a positive self-image and self-esteem is crucial for personal growth and aligning with one's true identity.

Chapter Summaries / Endnotes / References:

4. **Beliefs and Limiting Beliefs**:
   - Beliefs shape our experiences and perceptions of the world and are often defended fiercely even against contrary evidence.
   - Limiting beliefs create barriers that prevent exploring new opportunities and realizing full potential.

5. **Origins of Limiting Beliefs**:
   - Childhood experiences and interactions with significant individuals shape our self-beliefs and internal dialogue.
   - Negativity bias causes us to remember negative experiences more than positive ones, impacting self-perception.

6. **Building Self-Esteem**:
   - Self-affirmations are powerful tools for enhancing self-esteem and fostering a positive self-image.
   - Regular practice of self-affirmations leads to better performance, greater pride, and a more confident outlook on life.

7. **Understanding and Aligning with Values**:
   - Values are the emotional states one wants to consistently experience
   - Living congruently with one's values ensures enduring happiness and aligns actions with personal principles and goals.

8. **Mastering Values**:

   o Differentiating between hedonistic values (immediate gratification) and meaning values (long-term fulfillment) aids in making decisions that align with one's true self.

   o Choosing meaningful values often involves enduring short-term discomfort for long-term benefits and overall well-being.

References:

1. https://www.psychologytoday.com/us/basics/identity

2. https://www.simplypsychology.org/self-concept.html

3. https://www.briantracy.com/blog/

4. https://positivepsychology.com/self-perception-theory/

5. https://www.psychologytoday.com/us/basics/limiting-beliefs

6. https://www.verywellmind.com/how-to-build-self-esteem-4163098

7. https://www.verywellmind.com/what-are-values-2795083

8. https://positivepsychology.com/hedonic-treadmill/

Here are some references on Maori philosophy and identity:

1. Connor, H. D. (2019). Whakapapa Back: Mixed Indigenous Māori and Pākehā Genealogy and Heritage in Aotearoa/New Zealand. Genealogy, 3(4), 73. https://www.mdpi.com/2313-5778/3/4/73

2. Harmsworth, G., & Tahi, M. (2008). Indigenous Maori Knowledge and Perspectives of Ecosystems. Landcare Research.

3. Royal, T. A. C. (2012). Politics and Knowledge: Kaupapa Maori and Matauranga Maori. Te Puni Kōkiri.

4. Ministry for the Environment. (2020). Te Ao Māori – Māori world view. Ministry for the Environment.

5. Durie, M. (1998). Whaiora: Māori Health Development. Google Books.

Chapter Four: Fears

In this chapter, we delved into the nature of fear, exploring its biological roots in the amygdala and its psychological impact on our lives. Fear, while a natural survival mechanism, often holds us back from pursuing our true potential and living authentically.

We discussed how fear manifests in different forms—realistic fears, action-required fears, and inner-state fears—and how these can inhibit our growth and decision-making.

Key strategies for overcoming fear were presented, including embracing vulnerability, practicing mindfulness, and setting realistic goals. The chapter emphasized the importance of acknowledging and understanding our fears rather than suppressing them, as well as the role of courage in taking action despite fear. Through case stories like Michael's journey to embrace vulnerability and John's battle with toxic habits, we saw how confronting fear head-on can lead to personal and relational transformation.

Endnotes

1. "Eckhart Tolle On The Origin of Fear and How To Overcome It," The Joy Within, December 16, 2019. Available at: The Joy Within. www.thejoywithin.org/authors/eckhart-tolle/the-origin-of-fear

3. "The Power of Now by Eckhart Tolle," Internet Archive. Available at: Internet Archive.

4. Shetty, J. (2020). *Think Like a Monk: Train Your Mind for Peace and Purpose Every Day.* Simon & Schuster.

5. "The Power of Now by Eckhart Tolle - Self Drive Psychology," Self Drive Psychology. Available at: Self Drive Psychology. www.selfdrivepsychology.com/the-power-of-now-by-eckhart-tolle

6. Pearson, S. (Year). *Your Success: 10 Steps to an Extraordinary Life.* Publisher.

7. Willson, R., & Branch, R. (Year). *Cognitive Behavioral Therapy for Dummies.* Publisher.

8. "Do One Thing Every Day That Scares You" - Eleanor Roosevelt. Available at: Goodreads.

Chapter Five: Character

In this chapter, we explore the critical role that character plays in achieving lasting success and personal fulfillment. Character is not just a trait of the successful but the very foundation upon which all meaningful achievements are built. Through the lens of personal development, we examine how daily habits, self-reflection, and the ability to navigate adversity shape our character over time.

The chapter introduces practical steps for cultivating a strong character, including the importance of complimenting others, modelling excellence, and building self-trust. We also discuss the significance of daily rituals in reinforcing discipline and aligning actions with long-term goals. Drawing on real-life examples, such as the New Zealand All Blacks rugby team and personal experiences from the author's life, the chapter underscores that character is forged through consistent effort, resilience, and a commitment to growth. The chapter concludes with an inspirational message, reminding readers that character is built through the choices they make every day and that embracing this journey is key to unlocking their true potential.

Endnotes

1. **John Hays Hammond Quote:**

Source: The quote "Character is the real foundation of all worthwhile success" is attributed to John Hays Hammond, an American mining engineer and philanthropist known for his contributions to the field of mining and his advocacy for the importance of character in leadership.

2. **Henry David Thoreau Quote:**

Source: The quote "You cannot dream yourself into a character; you must hammer and forge yourself one" is from Henry David Thoreau, a renowned American essayist, poet, and philosopher, emphasizing the active effort required to build character.

3. **Jim Rohn on Personal Development:**

Source: Jim Rohn, a prominent American entrepreneur, author, and motivational speaker, often spoke about personal development being the foundation of success, including the idea that "Success is something you attract by the person you become."

4. **Legacy by James Kerr:**

Reference: Kerr, J. (2013). *Legacy: What the All Blacks Can Teach Us About the Business of Life*. London: Constable & Robinson. This book explores the character-building practices of the New Zealand All Blacks rugby team, including the principle of "Sweep the Shed."

How to Win Friends and Influence People by Dale Carnegie:
Reference: Carnegie, D. (1936). *How to Win Friends and Influence People*. New York: Simon & Schuster. This classic book discusses the importance of character and self-perception in achieving success and influencing others.

5. **The Power of Habit by Charles Duhigg:**

Reference: Duhigg, C. (2012). *The Power of Habit: Why We Do What We Do in Life and Business*. New York: Random House. This book explains how habits shape our lives and how establishing positive routines can lead to significant personal and professional growth.

6. **Atomic Habits by James Clear:**

Reference: Clear, J. (2018). *Atomic Habits: An Easy & Proven Way to Build Good Habits & Break Bad Ones*. New York: Avery. Clear's book emphasizes the transformative power of small, consistent actions and the importance of daily rituals in achieving long-term success.

7. **Jay Shetty on Daily Rituals:**

Source: Shetty, J. (2020). *Think Like a Monk: Train Your Mind for Peace and Purpose Every Day*. New York: Simon & Schuster. Shetty discusses the importance of daily rituals such as making your bed to cultivate discipline and mindfulness.

Chapter Summaries / Endnotes / References:

8. Personal Experience:

Reference: The author's personal journey from school dropout to performing arts achiever highlights the importance of character building through discipline, feedback, and perseverance. These experiences

underscore the broader themes of the chapter, illustrating the real-world application of the principles discussed.

Chapter Six: Trauma

In this chapter, we explore the profound impact trauma can have on our lives and the healing journey required to break free from its grip. Trauma, whether from childhood experiences, relationships, or life events, often shapes our emotional responses, behaviors, and perceptions in ways that limit our potential. Through understanding how trauma manifests and acknowledging its influence, we can begin the process of healing and reclaiming control over our lives.

The chapter delves into the stages of healing, encouraging you to confront unhealed wounds with courage and compassion. You'll discover how trauma often creates protective layers, distorting our true selves and leading to patterns of fear, pain, and self-sabotage. By peeling back these layers, we learn to reconnect with our core, embracing vulnerability as a path to healing. Personal stories, practical tools, and psychological insights guide you in breaking free from the cycles of trauma, allowing you to move forward with greater resilience and clarity. Healing is not about erasing the past but transforming it, allowing you to step into a more empowered, authentic version of yourself.

Endnotes

1. Maté, Gabor. When the Body Says No: Exploring the Stress-Disease Connection. John Wiley & Sons, 2003.

2. Australian Psychological Society. "Understanding and Managing Trauma". Accessed June 26, 2024.

3. Brown, Brené. The Gifts of Imperfection: Let Go of Who You Think You're Supposed to Be and Embrace Who You Are. Hazelden Publishing, 2010.

4. Pearson, Remi. The Coaching Institute: Core, Crud, Crust Model. Accessed June 26, 2024.

5. Cooley, Charles H. Human Nature and the Social Order. Scribner's, 1902.

6. Remi Pearson, previously known as Sharon Pearson, changed her name as part of her personal and professional transformation. She is the founder of The Coaching Institute in 2004, This name change reflects her evolution and deeper connection to her true self. For more details, visit her official website and The Coaching Institute (The Coaching Institute) (BraveHeart) (The Coaching Institute) (The Coaching Institute).

7. For more insights on Gabor Maté's perspectives on trauma, you might find his books "When the Body Says No" and "The Body Keeps the Score" helpful.

Chapter Summaries / Endnotes / References:

The concept of emotional intelligence (EI) was popularized by Daniel Goleman, an American psychologist, in his 1995 book *Emotional Intelligence: Why It Can Matter More Than IQ*. However, the term "emotional intelligence" was first introduced by researchers Peter Salovey and John D. Mayer in their 1990 article titled "Emotional Intelligence." They defined it as the ability to monitor one's own and others' emotions, to discriminate among them, and to use this information to guide one's thinking and actions.

Amato, P. R. (2000). The consequences of divorce for adults and children. *Journal of Marriage and Family, 62*(4), 1269-1287.

American Psychiatric Association. (2013). *Diagnostic and statistical manual of mental disorders* (5th ed.). Washington, DC: Author.

American Psychological Association. (2020). Trauma. Retrieved from https://www.apa.org/topics/trauma

Australian Psychological Society. (2012). Understanding and managing trauma. Retrieved from https://www.psychology.org.au/for-the-public/Psychology-topics/Trauma

Bowlby, J. (1982). *Attachment and loss: Vol. 1. Attachment* (2nd ed.). New York: Basic Books.

Brown, B. (2012). *Daring greatly: How the courage to be vulnerable transforms the way we live, love, parent, and lead.* New York: Gotham.

Bryant, R. A. (2003). Early predictors of posttraumatic stress disorder. *Biological Psychiatry, 53*(9), 789-795.

Carhart-Harris, R. L., & Goodwin, G. M. (2017). The therapeutic potential of psychedelic drugs: Past, present, and future. *Neuropsychopharmacology, 42*(11), 2105-2113.

Carhart-Harris, R. L., Erritzoe, D., Williams, T., Stone, J. M., Reed, L. J., Colasanti, A., ... & Nutt, D. J. (2012). Neural correlates of the psychedelic state as determined by fMRI studies with psilocybin. *Proceedings of the National Academy of Sciences, 109*(6), 2138-2143.

Chamberlain, D. B. (1994). Babies remember birth: And other extraordinary scientific discoveries about the mind and personality of your newborn. *Inner Traditions/Bear & Co.*

Crittenden, P. M. (1992). Quality of attachment in the preschool years. *Development and Psychopathology, 4*(2), 209-241.

Cummings, E. M., & Davies, P. T. (1994). Children and marital conflict: The impact of family dispute and resolution. *Guilford Press.*

Davies, P. T., & Cummings, E. M. (1994). Marital conflict and child adjustment: An emotional security hypothesis. *Psychological Bulletin, 116*(3), 387-411.

Evans, G. W., & English, K. (2002). The environment of poverty: Multiple stressor exposure, psychophysiological stress, and socioemotional adjustment. *Child Development, 73*(4), 1238-1248.

Fals-Stewart, W., Kelley, M. L., & Fincham, F. D. (2004). Substance-abusing parents' attitudes towards allowing their children to participate in treatment: A comparison of mothers versus fathers. *Journal of Family Psychology, 18*(4), 666-671.

Finkelhor, D. (2008). *Childhood victimization: Violence, crime, and abuse in the lives of young people.* Oxford University Press.

Griffiths, R. R., Johnson, M. W., Carducci, M. A., et al. (2016). Psilocybin produces substantial and sustained decreases in depression and anxiety in patients with life-threatening cancer: A randomized double-blind trial. *Journal of Psychopharmacology,*

Chapter Summaries / Endnotes / References:

Chapter Seven: Relationships

This chapter explores the profound impact that father-son relationships, inherited patterns, and personal growth have on the development of healthy, fulfilling relationships. It emphasizes the importance of self-awareness and the power of perspective in breaking negative cycles, using real-life examples like the stories of Robert Downey Jr. and Donald Trump to illustrate how childhood experiences shape adult behavior.

Key insights from experts like Garrett J. White and John Gottman provide practical strategies for building and maintaining strong relationships, including the importance of integrity, effective communication, and stress management. The chapter also delves into the dynamics of feminine and masculine energies, highlighting how a balanced approach can enhance intimacy and connection.

By applying the strategies discussed, readers can transform their relationships, ensuring they become positive, supportive partners and fathers. The chapter concludes with a reminder that the journey towards healthier relationships begins with self-love, intentional choices, and the commitment to personal growth.

Endnotes

1. **Jim Rohn's Story**: Rohn, J. (2019). *Leading an Inspired Life*. Success Media.

2. **Garrett J. White's Quote and Perspective**: White, G. J. (2016). *Warrior Book: The Warrior's Way*. Wake Up Warrior.

3. **Tony Robbins' Quote**: Robbins, T. (2017). *Unshakeable: Your Financial Freedom Playbook*. Simon & Schuster.

4. **Robert Downey Jr.'s Story**: Gross, T. (2008, December 16). Robert Downey Jr.: The Fresh Air Interview. NPR. Retrieved from https://www.npr.org/templates/story/story.php?storyId=98305796

5. **Statistics on Fatherlessness**: National Fatherhood Initiative. (2017). *Father Facts*. Retrieved from https://www.fatherhood.org/father-absence-statistics. Fatherlessness and its effects on American society - America First Policy

6. **Effects of Trauma on Relationships**: American Psychological Association. (2018). Trauma's Toll on Relationships. Retrieved from https://www.apa.org/news/press/releases/2018/11/trauma-relationships

7. **Strategies for Personal Growth**: Cloud, H. (2013). *Boundaries: When to Say Yes, How to Say No to Take Control of Your Life*. Zondervan.

8. Donald Trump's childhood was significantly influenced by his father, Fred Trump, who was authoritarian and emotionally abusive. For detailed insights, refer to Mary Trump's book *Too Much and Never Enough: How My Family Created the World's Most*

Chapter Summaries / Endnotes / References:

10. *Dangerous Man.* Information is available on The Independent's website: The Independent.

11. Fred Trump's harsh treatment and emotional neglect caused Donald to view the world as hostile, always feeling the need to prove himself. This concept is discussed in the MIT Press Reader article: MIT Press Reader.

12. Mary Trump's book reveals how Fred's actions deprived Donald of the ability to experience a full range of human emotions. More information can be found in the same article from The Independent: The Independent.

13. Fred Trump's failure to provide emotional safety intensified Donald's emotional challenges. This topic is covered in depth on PACEs Connection: PACEs Connection.

14. Research indicates that a positive father figure plays a significant role in the emotional and psychological development of boys and men. For instance, studies have shown that supportive and involved fathering is linked to better social and cognitive outcomes for children. Positive father involvement contributes to higher self-esteem, better academic performance, and healthier social interactions in children (Lamb, M. E., 2010, *The Role of the Father in Child Development*).

15. The absence of a father or a negative father-son relationship can indeed contribute to various psychological issues. Research has consistently found that boys who grow up without a father or with an uninvolved father are at increased risk for a range of negative outcomes, including higher rates of aggression, behavioral problems, and difficulties in forming healthy relationships (McLanahan, S., & Sandefur, G., 1994, *Growing Up with a Single Parent: What Hurts, What Helps*).

16. Additionally, studies have linked father absence or disengagement to lower self-esteem and increased susceptibility to depression. For example, one study found that father absence was associated with higher levels of depressive symptoms in adolescents and young adults (Amato, P. R., 2001, *The Consequences of Divorce for Adults and Children*).

17. Men who experience problematic father-son relationships may face difficulties in their intimate relationships as adults. Research suggests that unresolved issues with fathers can lead to difficulties in forming and maintaining healthy romantic relationships, often due to issues of trust and attachment (Elder, G. H., 1998, *The Life Course as Developmental Theory*).

18. Addressing the emotional and psychological impacts of problematic father-son relationships can be crucial for improving mental and emotional wellbeing. Therapeutic approaches such as family therapy and counseling can help individuals address and work through these issues, potentially leading to healthier relationships and improved mental health

Chapter Summaries / Endnotes / References:

20. (Johnson, S. M., 2004, *The Practice of Emotionally Focused Couple Therapy: Creating Connection*).

21. **American Psychological Association (APA)**: The information on stress management strategies was sourced from the APA's guidelines and resources on managing stress effectively, which emphasize the importance of resilience and healthy coping mechanisms in maintaining both physical and mental health. More detailed information can be found on their website: www.apa.org/topic/stress

22. Deida, D. (1997). *The Way of the Superior Man: A Spiritual Guide to Mastering the Challenges of Women, Work, and Sexual Desire*. Sounds True.

23. David Deida's official website: https://deida.info/.

Chapter Eight: Language

In this chapter, we explore the profound impact language has on our perceptions, relationships, and overall life experience. Words are not merely tools for communication; they shape our reality and influence how we perceive and interact with the world. We discuss the power of how labels and how they can limit or expand our experiences, emphasizing the importance of choosing words that empower rather than restrict.

Whether in professional settings, parenting, or daily interactions, the chapter highlights the critical role of language in influencing those around us. By consciously selecting our words, we can transform ordinary statements into powerful affirmations that uplift and inspire.

The chapter also offers practical strategies for reframing negative language and thoughts into positive, empowering expressions. Through careful attention to the language we use, we can reshape our mindset, approach challenges with resilience, and unlock new possibilities in our lives. This chapter serves as a guide to harnessing the power of words, encouraging readers to start making intentional language choices today, and paving the way for greater personal and interpersonal growth.

Chapter Nine: Dreams

In this chapter, we delve into the transformative power of setting intentional and well-defined goals. The chapter emphasizes the importance of dreaming big and connecting deeply with your "why" to fuel daily actions and decisions. Through personal stories and examples, the chapter illustrates how perseverance and resilience are crucial in overcoming obstacles and setbacks on the journey to success.

Key concepts like the S.M.A.R.T. framework provide a practical approach to turning dreams into actionable plans, ensuring that your goals are Specific, Measurable, Attainable, Realistic, and Time-bound. The chapter also highlights the importance of focusing on one significant goal at a time to avoid goal overload and emphasizes that the true value lies not just in achieving your goals but in who you become in the process.

Keynotes:

- The power of dreaming big and using your vision to guide daily decisions.
- The importance of connecting with your "why" to stay motivated and overcome challenges.
- Practical application of the S.M.A.R.T framework for effective

Chapter Summaries / Endnotes / References:

goal setting.

- The significance of intentionality and prioritization in achieving meaningful goals.
- Personal growth and self-discovery as the ultimate rewards of pursuing goals.

References:

- Walt Disney's quote on the courage to pursue dreams.
- Christopher Howard's coaching insights on imagining and creating the greatest dream.
- Teachings from Dr. Joe Dispenza and motivational speaker Jim Rohn on connecting dreams to future goals.
- Simon Sinek's book *Start With Why* and its exploration of finding your core purpose.
- Sharon Pearson's perspective on raising standards when facing challenges, from her book *Your Success*.
- Brian Tracy's book *Goals* on the importance of having clear, written goals for success.
- Bob Proctor's teachings from *The Secret* on the power of visualization in goal attainment.

1. Jim Rohn
   https://www.youtube.com/watch?v=LFDD1fhVeOY
2. Sean Patrick Flanery is an American actor and author known for his roles in films such as "The Boondock Saints" and "Powder." He authored the memoir "Tales of the American: The Story of a Man Who Wanted to Do Better," which reflects on his life experiences and personal growth.

Chapter Ten: Visualising

In this final chapter, we explored the powerful practice of visualization and how it serves as the bridge between dreams and reality. By now, you have developed a stronger sense of self, a healthier self-image, and a renewed level of self-belief. With these tools in hand, your goals and aspirations have likely evolved, becoming clearer and more aligned with your true desires.

We delved into the mechanics of visualization, including the importance of goal and process visualization, and how engaging your senses and emotions can make your visions more vivid and achievable. We also addressed common obstacles that might arise, such as negative self-talk, difficulty maintaining focus, and skepticism, and provided strategies to overcome these challenges. Additionally, we examined the profound connection between the heart and brain, emphasizing how internal transformation can lead to external success. Whether in the context of individual goals or collective efforts like those seen in the Te Matatini Kapa Haka competitions, the power of aligned energy and intention cannot be overstated.

As you move forward, remember that the journey of self-discovery and growth does not end here.

The insights and practices you've gained throughout this book are tools you can continue to refine and apply in your life. Visualization is not a one-time event but a continuous practice that evolves as you do. By consistently applying the principles of visualization, self-belief, and intentional action, you can create a life that reflects your deepest values and aspirations.

Book Cover Design: Anze Ban V from Slovenia @topcreativemind

Chapter Summaries / Endnotes / References:

About the Author

Devlin Tikitiki is a seasoned tour director, mindset coach, and storyteller who has guided thousands across the breathtaking landscapes of Australia and Aotearoa, New Zealand. With over three decades of experience working with people from all walks of life, Devlin brings a powerful blend of lived wisdom, from his time as a high school teacher at the age of 25 to being an Assistant Cruise Director with Princess Cruises at the age of 30. His cultural grounding, and emotional intelligence are only a few aspects to assists with his life coaching work. Devlin was raised in a minority community marked by poverty, addiction, and adversity.

The Path Ahead

He survived childhood abuse, left school early, and spent his youth navigating environments that could have broken him but through grit, healing, and self-reflection, Devlin began rewriting his story—overcoming limiting beliefs, educating himself, and rising to become a certified NLP practitioner and mindset mastery coach.

His journey—from trauma to transformation, from silence to self-expression—is a powerful testament to the healing potential of inner work and cultural connection. Whether he's performing haka as a form of release, participating in ancient healing retreats, meditating at sunrise on the shores of Circular Quay, or guiding men to reclaim their purpose,

Devlin's mission remains clear: to live a life of excellence while helping others rise above their circumstances and live with clarity, courage, and compassion. When he's not leading tours or empowering others, Devlin can be found grounding himself in nature, sharing laughter with community, or crafting content that speaks straight to the heart.

Printed in Great Britain
by Amazon